Lao Close Encounters

Lao Close Encounters

John J.S. Burton

Orchid Press

John J.S. Burton
LAO CLOSE ENCOUNTERS

ORCHID PRESS
P.O. Box 19,
Yuttitham Post Office,
Bangkok 10907, Thailand

www.orchidbooks.com

Copyright © 2005 Orchid Press
All rights reserved

Front cover: An Asiatic water buffalo, *Bubalus bubalis*, the shy, inquisitive work animal of the rice fields
The encircled LAO design is the sticker issued by the government for Lao-registered vehicles undertaking international travel.

End papers: Woven Houa Phan wall hanging, the best souvenir with no two the same

Half title: Woven Houa Phan wall hanging

Back cover: Villages just above Luang Prabang have strong weaving traditions; both the technique and the products are on display.

Spine: The *khaen* is quintessential among Lao instruments.

Photographs are by the author unless otherwise credited in the captions.

Printed in Thailand

ISBN 974-524-075-3

TABLE OF CONTENTS

INTRODUCTION 1
   Maps and Signs 1
   Tourists 2
   Souvenirs 4
   Currency 6
   Law and Order 6
   Power Generation 7
VIENTIANE, SEAT OF GOVERNMENT 9
   Capital Sights 9
   Urban Problems 17
   Vientiane Capital 21
INTERNATIONAL HERITAGE 22
   French Legacy 22
   Russian Legacy 24
   Legacy of War 25
   Aid Donors 30
LIFE 31
   Spiritual Matters 31
   Children 39
   School 41
   Weddings and Baci 42
   Recreation 42
   Entertainment 47
   Music 48
   Food 50
   Festivals 54
   Tribal Life 62
   Death 66
AGRICULTURE AND FORESTRY 67
   Rice Is Life Is Rice 67
   Fish Farming and Fishing 72
   Vegetables 75
   Fruit 79
   Poppies 81
   Domestic Animals 82
   Silviculture 86
   The Forest 87
   The Forest Harvested 88
   Post-Harvest Losses 89
   Slash-and-Burn 90
OTHER INTERESTING OCCUPATIONS 92
   Mulberries 92
   Mulberry Paper 93
   Kapok 96
   Brooms 97
   Horticulture 98
   Construction 101
   Bamboo, Rattan, Wickerwork 103
   Woodworking 104
   Distilling 106
   Carpetmaking 107
   Weaving 108
   Brickmaking 111
   Factory Hands 112
   Traveling Salesmen 113
   Jewelers, Silversmiths 114
   Artists 115
TRAVEL 116
   Travel by Air 116
   Travel by Water 117
   Mekong River 119
   Travel by Rail 122
   Travel by Road 123
NATURE 130
   Flora 130
   Fauna 136
THE PROVINCES 144
   Attapeu Province 144
   Bokeo Province 147
   Bolikhamsai Province 150
   Champasak Province 154
   Houa Phan Province 160
   Khammouan Province 164
   Luang Nam Tha Province 168
   Luang Prabang Province 173
   Oudomsai Province 181
   Phongsali Province 184
   Saisomboun Special Zone 189
   Salavan Province 192
   Savannakhet Province 195
   Sayabouli Province 199
   Sekong Province 205
   Sieng Khouang Province 208
   Vientiane Province 213
CONCLUSION 219
INDEX 220

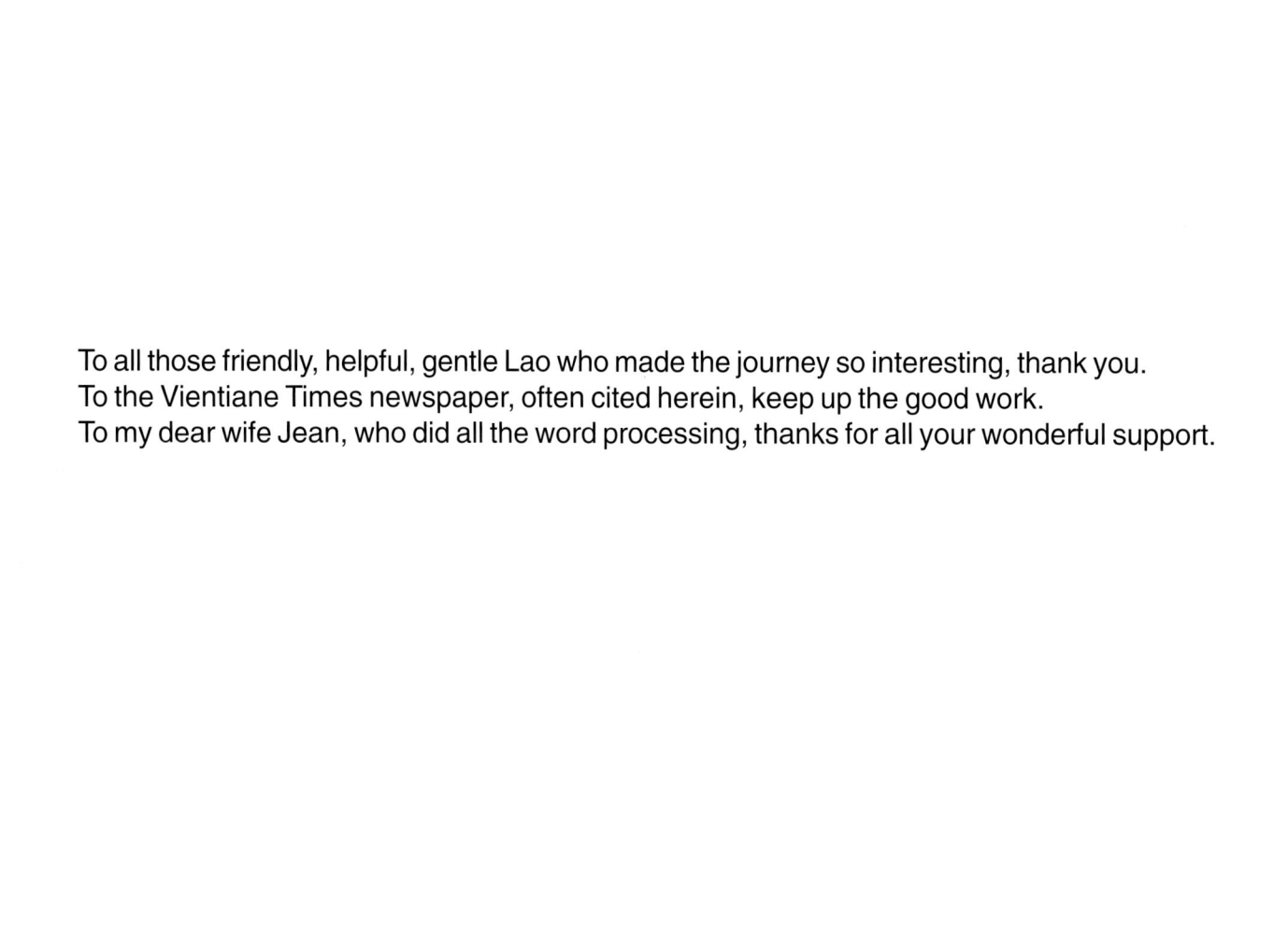

To all those friendly, helpful, gentle Lao who made the journey so interesting, thank you.
To the Vientiane Times newspaper, often cited herein, keep up the good work.
To my dear wife Jean, who did all the word processing, thanks for all your wonderful support.

Laos is an extraordinary country of six million people with many recent events putting it "on the map:" successful hosting of the Association of Southeast Asian Nations (ASEAN) Summit, surging road and bridge construction underway including a Thailand-China highway link and a new Mekong River bridge between Mukdahan, Thailand, and Savannakhet, Laos, upgrading of Wattay International Airport (Vientiane) to accommodate Boeing 747s, Normal Trade Relations (NTR) with Laos signed into law in the U.S.A., visa exemptions for citizens of ASEAN countries, and even the opening of the first supermarket. December 2005 marks 30 years of the Lao People's Democratic Republic.

There are various good guidebooks to Laos; this does not compete with them. It recommends no restaurants or places to stay, no brand names or establishments to patronize, and no schedules to follow. Instead it is a pictorial journey around the country to see the things for which there never seems to be enough time or resources or suitable weather. It is also a portrait of Laos as it exists now, preserved for the future when rapid change will have altered the way life is lived here.

The basic nature of the people is friendly and welcoming, whether they are lowland Lao or tribal highlanders. Laos is a treasure for anyone who is interested in natural history, as the population pressure on the environment is still relatively light. Travel is constrained not by the government but by road hazards and lack of facilities. But whatever its problems, risks, or deprivations, Laos is a country to be experienced.

The author joins the Bolikhamsai provincial government in wishing you a happy trip, whether it is through Laos or simply through these pages.

INTRODUCTION
Maps and Signs. There are a number of maps available, none of them particularly accurate with respect to presence, absence, or alignment of minor roads. This map (left) is the government's own, available from the Lao National Geographic Service. It has the advantage of showing the location of all of the 141 district (*muang*) towns, where services are most likely to be available. It is the map upon which all of the District identifications in the photo captions are based. An outline map may also be bought as a T-shirt (below left). If you see a Kaysone Phomvihane memorial pavilion like this one (below right), you are in a district town, and nearly every district has one.

Introduction

Directional road signs along main roads are on the increase, while those on country roads are still sparse or entirely lacking. The same is true of place name signs. Place names have meaning, some of them quite memorable, such as this one in Champasak Province (right) which means "water buffalo blood stream." The transliteration of Lao script is inconsistent, as shown by these two signs (below left and below right) occurring at the same site along Route 13S in Bolikhamsai Province, one for the stream and one for the adjacent village. The signs show "hand washing stream" though there is not a drop of water present in the dry season.

Tourists. Maps and signs in the Roman alphabet, whether or not they are transliterated consistently, are most welcome by international visitors who come from all over. They may come at age 2 (below left, on Champasak ferry), as teenagers (below right, at Buddha Park outside Vientiane), or as senior citizens (right, at Phoukhoun, southern Luang Prabang Province). Some of them are remarkably self-reliant, though this is not a requirement. They come for the natural environment, the culture, the sightseeing and exercise, to buy souvenirs, and for the sheer adventure of it all.

Thai visitors may come over in their own futuristic tour buses, such as this one (above) at the Morning Market, Vientiane.

Lao Close Encounters

One of the things that facilitated tourism was the construction of the Friendship Bridge from Nong Khai, Thailand (above), to Tha Deua near Vientiane, Laos (above right), in 1994. Another was gaining membership in the Association of Southeast Asian Nations (ASEAN) in 1997. But what really flung the doors wide open to tourism was the government's "Visit Laos Year 1999-2000" campaign (below). Official statistics show that tourist arrivals went from 14,400 in 1990 to 620,000 in 2003 (Vientiane Times, 12 April 2004), exceeding the electricity industry as the country's number one source of foreign currency. Long gone are the days when, "For traveling outside the Vientiane Province it is absolutely necessary to obtain a laissez-passes (travel permit) from the authorities…Failure to do so will certainly result in arrest and very uncomfortable deportation procedures" (quoted from a 1994 government provincial tourist map of Luang Prabang). Thai visitors lead the rest by far, followed by Vietnam and the U.S.A.

Even easier: now a single direct bus (left) can be taken from Udornthani, Thailand, to downtown Vientiane. Three more Thai-Lao direct routes have been announced for 2006.

There are a number of locally produced periodicals in English (right) that are sources of information for visitors and residents alike.

Introduction

Souvenirs. Wall hangings are readily available, portable, and attractive. A single one nicely fills a particular space (far left), while an array may serve as a photogenic backdrop (center left).

The wooden hangers are an art form in their own right, and can be found in the correct size for any hangings. The best ones are from the Luang Prabang area (below), here portraying elephants, *phayanak*, and *nok hong*.

Silver and gold jewelry is available in many places. The largest selection may be upstairs in the Morning Market in Vientiane (below), but small craft shops do a credible job (below right).

Lao Close Encounters

Woodcraft (top left) and pottery (center left) are both appealing, albeit a bit more cumbersome for travelers; a salesgirl models the T-shirt (left) that tourists most often purchase; all Vientiane.

Hmong ethnic crafts are distinctive and practical, as seen here at the annual Women's International Group bazaar, Vientiane (right); and salespersons of any age can be very persuasive (above right) in the Luang Prabang market.

Introduction

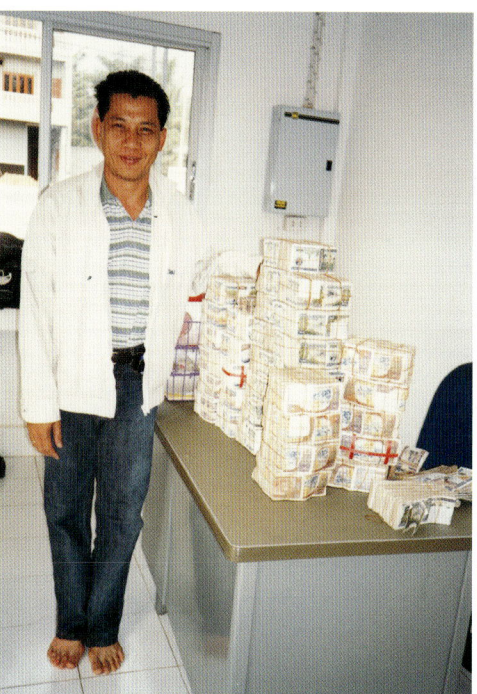

Currency. Although Thai baht and U.S. dollars are often accepted in the Mekong River valley including the major tour destinations, the country's currency is the kip. At present the most convenient quick calculation for which you would not be too far wrong is to move the decimal point four places to the left to convert kip to U.S. dollars. Until 2002, the largest kip denomination was 5000, but now there are 10,000 and 20,000 kip notes if you can find them (above left). For the business owner who has a high cash flow, this means dealing with "bales" of money (above right).

Law and Order. Social order is maintained by the police and military forces. In an urban setting such as Vientiane, the police do not usually have an active role in directing traffic, but they are on hand in case there is an accident or traffic violation at their assigned corner (far left). The soldiers cover the countryside (center left), Champasak Province. Laos currently enjoys very good relations with all five of its neighbors, so if soldiers are active it is an internal question. On special occasions such as That Luang Festival, Vientiane, the citizenry may be called upon to assist in maintaining order; in this case the older students lend a hand (above).

6   Lao Close Encounters

This billboard-size version of Lao military readiness is sponsored by a Lao-Chinese joint venture company.

Power Generation. This subject comes right up front because development is dependent on it, and it is the number two source of income, trailing only the tourist industry since 2002 (Vientiane Times, 5 October 2004). The main hydroelectric dam in the country is on the Nam Ngoum River in Keo-Oudom District of Vientiane Province (right). Built in the late 1960s and financed by the World Bank and various donor nations, it backs up an enormous reservoir, a good destination for a day trip which may also include a visit to the zoo.

Other hydroelectric projects include the Nam Thoen River Dam (upstream face shown above) in Bolikhamsai Province; the Nam Tha 3 Dam outside Luang Nam Tha (left); the Nam Phao River works in Khamkeut District of Bolikhamsai Province (above right); and the Nam Ngai River Dam north of Hatsa, Khoa District, Phongsali Province (right). Altogether there are about 46 hydropower projects of various sizes in the country (Vientiane Times, 1 October 2004).

Introduction

The day that electricity poles finally arrive in a village must be a special occasion for all. Poles are being erected (above) in a village in Sangthong District, Vientiane Province.

In the meantime, villagers use candles. If they live near a fast-flowing stream, they may have their own generator in the water such as the ones (above) in Khamkeut District, Bolikhamsai Province, connected to the house by a wire that is capable of lighting one bulb. Solar panels such as this one (left) in Khong District, Champasak Province, are as yet rarely seen.

In addition to power generation and distribution, the government, through its various ministries, implements numerous other development programs including infrastructure projects (note urban renewal and park development, above), health (note dengue fever prevention poster, below), education, natural resource management, and poverty reduction, to name just a few; Vientiane.

VIENTIANE, SEAT OF GOVERNMENT

Capital Sights. As both the seat of government and the center of the tourist industry, there is a great deal to do and see in Vientiane. But what is Vientiane? On the one hand, it is a city made up of several administrative districts that are in turn broken down into a series of villages, such as the one with its sign (above left). On the other hand it is a capital territory consisting of 9 districts and measuring about 110 kilometers from its western to its eastern extremities, parts of which are entirely rural. In Lao language the capital territory is called "Kamphaeng Nakhon" as shown on the license plate (above center), but translating this seems problematic. The sign outside the area's seat of government still shows Vientiane Prefecture (above right), but it has gone through two changes of name in recent years, being known for a time as Vientiane Municipality and now as Vientiane Capital. Kamphaeng Nakhon literally means city wall, and a portion of the real outer city wall, of considerable antiquity, has recently been excavated for public view to the southeast of the city (center left). The Fountain Circle (Nam Phou) is a major downtown landmark (center right); thoroughly renovated in 2002, those who saw it before will remember a less manicured but much shadier site.

The greater affluence of the city can be measured by the sea of motorbikes parked at schools waiting to take their student owners home (below left). Farther out, it's still predominantly bicycles (below center). Just the same, some things in Vientiane are still done quite traditionally (below right).

Vientiane, Seat of Government

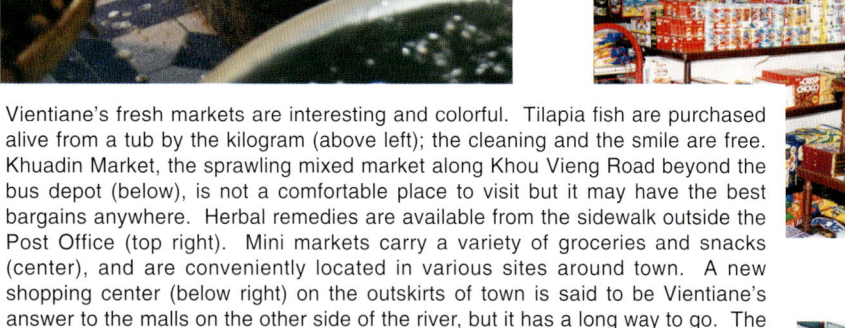

Vientiane's fresh markets are interesting and colorful. Tilapia fish are purchased alive from a tub by the kilogram (above left); the cleaning and the smile are free. Khuadin Market, the sprawling mixed market along Khou Vieng Road beyond the bus depot (below), is not a comfortable place to visit but it may have the best bargains anywhere. Herbal remedies are available from the sidewalk outside the Post Office (top right). Mini markets carry a variety of groceries and snacks (center), and are conveniently located in various sites around town. A new shopping center (below right) on the outskirts of town is said to be Vientiane's answer to the malls on the other side of the river, but it has a long way to go. The new but distant "super mart" (center right) is the first of its kind in the country, but it likewise has a long way to go to meet the competition across the river.

10   Lao Close Encounters

The Morning Market (above) is an important focal point of interest and it may take some time to see all of its lanes in three main buildings, including upstairs. Its name is no longer entirely descriptive, as it is now open until 4:30 pm.

Nowhere is the contrast between the traditional and the modern more apparent than in the Ethnic Handicrafts Center across the street from the Morning Market, where a single small booth (above right) may be draped with handmade weavings for sale, while at the same time the equipment is available for any grandmother to stop in and make a computer phone call to her relatives overseas. The Central Post Office (center right) is also across the street from the Morning Market. Stamp collectors will be pleased.

The Victory Gate (Patusai), patterned on the Arc de Triomphe, was formerly called simply The Monument (Anousawali); people with very long memories have reason to nickname it The Vertical Runway. By night (below left) or by day (below right) it is an impressive structure. An explanatory plaque (left) appears at the entrance.

Vientiane, Seat of Government

Overviews of the capital city can be had by climbing to the top of Patusai: looking southeast (top left); looking northeast (above); and looking southwest toward the Presidential Palace (top right). Even if you choose not to climb any stairs at all at the Patusai monument, the view of the dome from the ground level is very striking (right). Proudest day: flags of the Association of Southeast Asian Nations and its Dialogue Partners fly over Vientiane on the occasion of the successful hosting of the 10th Summit in November 2004 (below).

Lao Close Encounters

The Presidential Palace (top), site of important meetings with visiting dignitaries, stands at the Mekong River end of the avenue from the Patusai monument. Mahosot, the principal public hospital (above), strives continually to raise its standards. The new headquarters of the Mekong River Commission (below), formerly in Phnom Penh, was ready for the arrival of its staff in July 2004.

The National Cultural Hall (above) is the venue for events staged for the public, such as an end-of-year school children's performance (below) and a Middle Eastern dance revue for which the dancers made a dramatic entrance through the audience (bottom).

Vientiane, Seat of Government

If you can't wait for an infrequent free show at the National Cultural Hall, then for a price these fine performers (above) will be happy to put on a very good cultural show for you at a downtown venue almost any night of the year, and you can try out your "*lamwong*" national dancing style at the end.

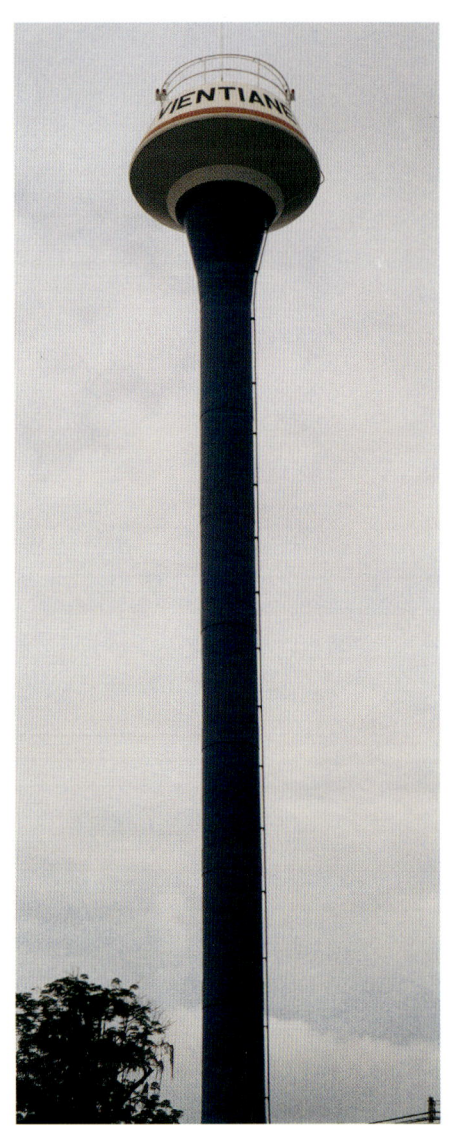

The "Vientiane" water tower (above) at the International Airport dominates Wat Tay village.

Landscaping of the capital's twelve parks is at a high standard, as evidenced at the 23 August Park (far left) and at Patuxay (Patusai) Park (near left); but one thing that is sometimes lacking is shade.

Lao Close Encounters

King Fa Ngoum, founder of the Lan Sang (Lane Xang) Kingdom, gives directions to his subjects (above). The statue is at the northwest end of the downtown business district. King Sisavangvong holds a palm leaf manuscript (below). His statue is just beyond Si Muang Temple at the southeast end of downtown.

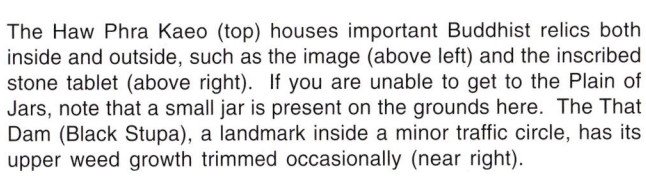

The Haw Phra Kaeo (top) houses important Buddhist relics both inside and outside, such as the image (above left) and the inscribed stone tablet (above right). If you are unable to get to the Plain of Jars, note that a small jar is present on the grounds here. The That Dam (Black Stupa), a landmark inside a minor traffic circle, has its upper weed growth trimmed occasionally (near right).

Vientiane, Seat of Government

15

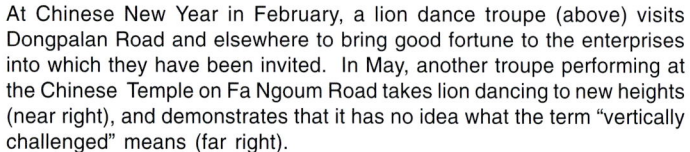

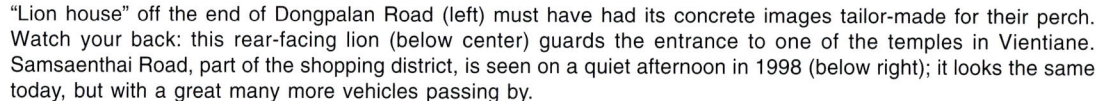

At Chinese New Year in February, a lion dance troupe (above) visits Dongpalan Road and elsewhere to bring good fortune to the enterprises into which they have been invited. In May, another troupe performing at the Chinese Temple on Fa Ngoum Road takes lion dancing to new heights (near right), and demonstrates that it has no idea what the term "vertically challenged" means (far right).

"Lion house" off the end of Dongpalan Road (left) must have had its concrete images tailor-made for their perch. Watch your back: this rear-facing lion (below center) guards the entrance to one of the temples in Vientiane. Samsaenthai Road, part of the shopping district, is seen on a quiet afternoon in 1998 (below right); it looks the same today, but with a great many more vehicles passing by.

Lao Close Encounters

The battle deescalates: in place of the previously aggressive "frackle-wart killing" (above), there is now simply "removal" (below). The English remains fractured.

Urban Problems. Traffic lights: Vientiane now has them at about twenty intersections; they may not be round (top, near right) and they may be more white than red (top, far right), but they still mean "stop." "Chin up" is a positive attitude toward life, but around here it's best to glance down frequently to avoid holes where drain covers are missing (below left). And speaking of drainage, the water in some places has nowhere to go after a storm, but the schoolchildren seem to take it all in stride (right). Additional drainpipes being laid under the streets in early 2005 (above) should alleviate this problem downtown. House fires are a sad story, often with nothing left to douse but ashes (bottom right) due to slow response time and peculiar debates about whether or not the appropriate authorities have turned off the electricity so as to make it safe to proceed. The walls in such a humid environment quickly become dark with fungal staining, and need to be whitewashed often (below), especially before important events like international conferences.

Vientiane, Seat of Government

Best walk in town: follow the river road downstream from town until you reach the grass-topped water tower (far left), then pass around behind it and cross the narrow steel bridge for a stroll through the friendly vegetable-growing village of Don Chan (center left). You can try out your first "*sabaai dee*" greetings here. But hurry up: a 14-story hotel complex (above), has already eaten up the upstream end of this rich river bottom farmland, and much more is planned.

The capital offers sublime accommodation complete with London taxi for the most discriminating tastes (below left). On the other hand it offers simple, breezy guest houses down leafy lanes at very inexpensive rates (below).

Lao Close Encounters

The National Museum (above) has a variety of subject material on display, but it is first and foremost the story of the revolutionary struggle and its successful conclusion.

The Kaysone Phomvihane Museum (above right) is located on the northeastern outskirts of town. Dedicated to the late President and Secretary General of the Lao People's Revolutionary Party, it is a grandiose structure with sparse exhibits and with no English captions. The statuary outside depicts the revolution in progress (left) and, presumably, the subsequent prosperity (center right).

The main campus of the National University of Laos is at Dong Dok, about 10 kilometers north of the town area. The new entrance (below left) leads to the administration building, while the old entrance (below right) is general purpose.

Vientiane, Seat of Government

"Buddha Park," downriver from the Friendship Bridge, is a peculiar assemblage of Buddhist and Hindu concrete statuary: an enormous reclining Buddha (left); monks touring the premises (right); getting a lot of things done at once (below); and a grasshopper (below right) that could rightly use the cliche "you're pulling my leg."

Women have an important role in this semi-matriarchal society, including educators (Dean of the Faculty of Science, National University of Laos, below left), government officials (Director of the National Library, below center) and entrepreneurs alike (below right).

20　　Lao Close Encounters

Vientiane Capital. Its territory not only includes the city of Vientiane but actually stretches for more than 105 kilometers from Sangthong District in the west to Pak Ngum District in the east, and includes some very rural areas. Statuary may be encountered unexpectedly, such as on the way to Tat Moon Falls (above left). The Hinkhanna Falls is a popular picnic spot on weekends in the hot season (above right). A village-made stick bridge on the way to Hinkhanna would enable small farm tractors to get across to the fields (right). An elephant gains shade and food at the same time from a bamboo grove 5 kilometers outside of Ban Phialat, Sangthong District (below left). Pleasant boat rides can be had on the Nam Ngoum River (below right) which has its origin on the Sieng Khouang plateau and ultimately forms the eastern boundary of the Capital.

Vientiane, Seat of Government

INTERNATIONAL HERITAGE

French Legacy. The French were, of course, resented colonials, but if it were not for them the country would probably be a lot smaller today, especially in the north and west. They defended it with a series of forts that themselves would make an interesting study, including the ones shown here. The Muang Sing Fort in Luang Nam Tha Province (top left) is currently used by the Lao military, as is the Muang Pak Lai Fort in Sayabouli Province (center left). Some of the lettering on the portal of the Muang Boun Tai Fort, Phongsali Province, can almost still be read (above center). The compound is currently used for administrative offices. Some recent French visitors have arrived at it with original photographs of their fathers in military service there. The fort at Ou Tai, Nyot Ou District, Phongsali Province (top right and center right) is likewise used for administrative offices.

Fort Carnot, on the hilltop at Ban Houai Sai, Bokeo Province (below), is in military use.

In the French cemetery on the outskirts of Vientiane, European Christian and North African Muslim alike, having given their lives for the motherland, find their final resting place side by side (left and below). The demise of the French in Indochina resulted from their defeat at the hands of the Viet Minh at Dien Bien Phu (Theng), which is in Vietnam only about ten kilometers "as the crow flies" from Phongsali Province. The battle lasted from 13 March through 7 May 1954. A large number of the Vientiane gravestones show deaths between these dates.

Lao Close Encounters

French Indochinese architecture has come to be appreciated. There are numerous good examples of it remaining in Vientiane, such as the National Library (near right) and the newly restored Asian Development Bank (far right), and also in other major towns. The "French trees," along Khou Vieng Road with their bases whitewashed in a beautification campaign (center left), and growing outside Mahosot Hospital (center second left), were indeed planted by the French but are actually *Swietenia mahagoni*, mahogany native to the West Indies. The French extensively planted trees along Lao roads but the vast majority have long since been felled.

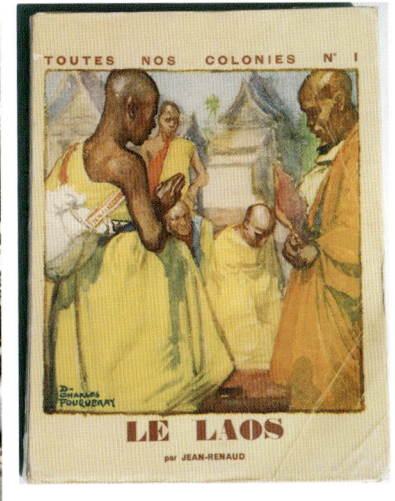

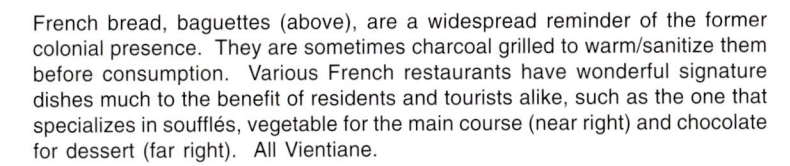

Judging from the cover of this well-illustrated 1930 book by Jean-Renaud, Laos was French Colony Number 1 (above left). The curious French game of petanque (above right), played with metal balls on a gravel court, still has its followers in major Mekong River towns. The Lao national team won at the Southeast Asian Games in 2001 and 2003.

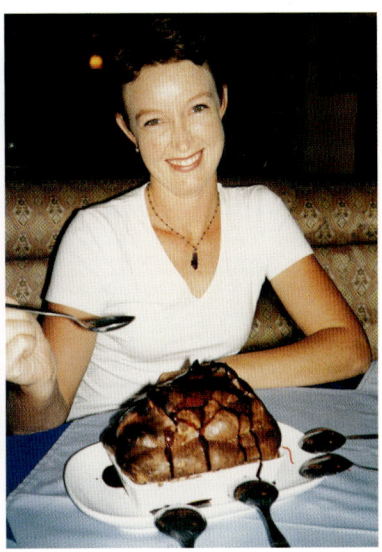

French bread, baguettes (above), are a widespread reminder of the former colonial presence. They are sometimes charcoal grilled to warm/sanitize them before consumption. Various French restaurants have wonderful signature dishes much to the benefit of residents and tourists alike, such as the one that specializes in soufflés, vegetable for the main course (near right) and chocolate for dessert (far right). All Vientiane.

International Heritage

Russian Legacy. The Vietnam "conflict" was also a battle of the superpowers, and the victorious revolutionaries persist in giving their "due" to the Soviets. Large portraits of Marx and Lenin hang in the Lao National Museum (above left), and the official government photograph of the most recent Party Congress (above right), which was held in 2001, still displays their likenesses on the facing curtain. To this day, the hammer-and-sickle flag of the Party may still be seen flying prominently together with the National flag (left), and Moscow is one of the time zones reported on the wall diagram at Wattay International Airport (right).

The Russian Circus, at the north side of Vientiane, is the venue for occasional performances (left). This government-owned hotel in Vientiane is from the Soviet era (right). The country's revolutionary leaders, though communist, acknowledged in 1986 that state-owned enterprises were not working particularly well for Lao people, and so created a "New Economic Mechanism" allowing for privatization. These abandoned government tobacco drying barns (below left) in northern Khammouan Province are testimony to the old system, while a privately owned tobacco field and drying barn (below right) represent the new way.

Lao Close Encounters

Legacy of War. The Americans chose to go to war in Vietnam in order to "stop the spread of international communism" in Asia. Treaties were signed to assure a neutral Laos, but it was not to be. From the beginning North Vietnamese Army (NVA) troops in their hundreds of thousands utilized Laos as a conduit to the south, developing tracks through the Lao forests which cumulatively came to be called the "Ho Chi Minh Trail" in the Western world. In the effort to deny them the use of Lao territory, and to support a non-communist government, the Americans conducted the most massive air bombardment in the history of mankind. Oft-cited statistics (e.g. USA Today, 12 December 2003; Vientiane Times, 5 November 2004) show that over 2 million tons of bombs were dropped on Laos in 580,000 sorties from 1960 to 1970, more than throughout all of Europe in World War II; and 12,000 Lao have died from accidents with unexploded ordnance from 1975 to date. Although hostilities ended 30 years ago, the repercussions are part and parcel of Lao life in large areas of the interior to this day.

The Se Banghiang River bridge at Ban Tat Hai village, Phin District, Savannakhet Province (above), and the Se Don River bridge west of Salavan town, Salavan Province (left), both on the interior road now identified as National Route 1, were bombed and never repaired or replaced, inhibiting commerce over a wide area. The shell of a downed American helicopter at Phin, Savannakhet Province (above left), is preserved as a reminder of the past.

International Heritage

Sepon (Tchepone) District of Savannakhet Province was at the heart of the Ho Chi Minh Trail, situated just west of the strategic North-South Vietnam divide of the 17th parallel, and it was here in the village of Ban Dong that "Operation Lamson 719" was staged. Army of the Republic of Vietnam (ARVN) troops, with American air support, invaded the Trail in a losing campaign that left tanks behind (above and right), being preserved by the government as reminders.

Equipment of the adversary: this is said to be a Chinese copy of a Russian T-54 tank on the trail from Dakchung District, Sekong Province, to Sansai District, Attapeu Province.

Lao Close Encounters

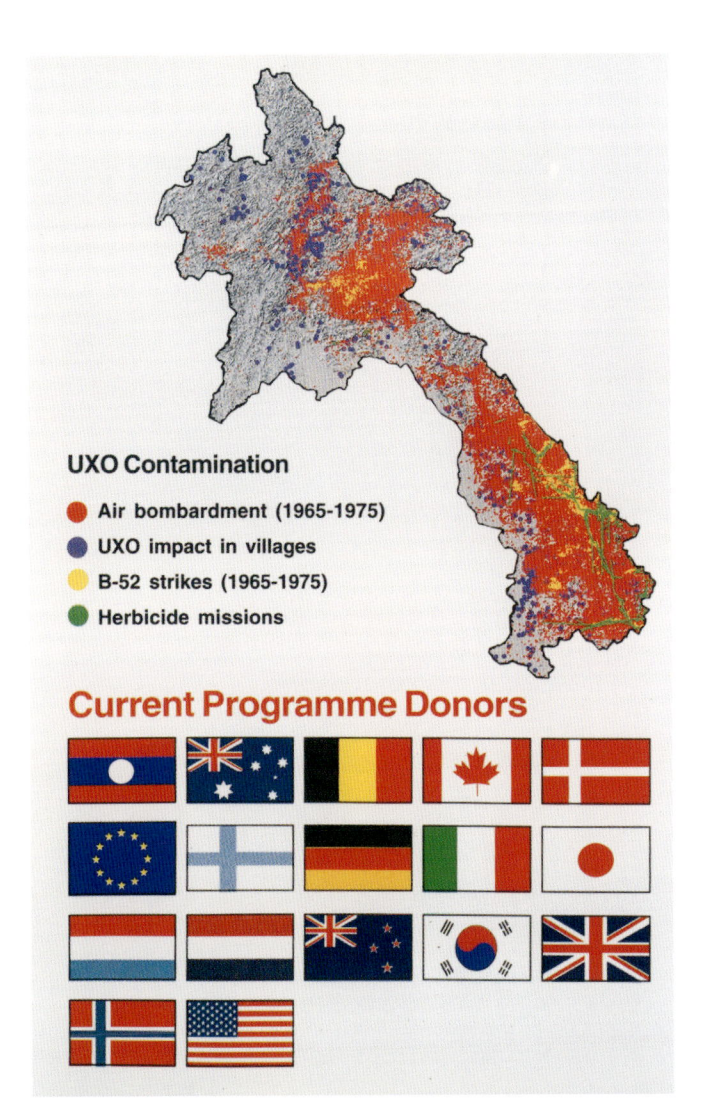

UXO Contamination
- 🔴 Air bombardment (1965-1975)
- 🔵 UXO impact in villages
- 🟡 B-52 strikes (1965-1975)
- 🟢 Herbicide missions

Current Programme Donors

The decade that the map turned red: UXO Lao is the organization responsible for the clearance of potentially dangerous remains (UXO=unexploded ordnance). Their map (left) shows that most of southeastern Laos beyond the Mekong River plain may be problematic until pronounced safe. The red blotch in the north, centered on the Plain of Jars, is not part of the Ho Chi Minh Trail, but was instead bombarded to contain indigenous revolutionary movements. Bomb clearance is a slow, expensive process. You may see UXO Lao trucks (above) operating in these areas. UXO danger signs such as this one in Paksong District, Champasak Province, are rarely seen. The average visitor is in no danger, as most of the ordnance is buried and would have to be struck or tampered with before detonation. The great majority of UXO accidents result from farming and scavenging activities.

This cluster bomb, or "bombie," has been unearthed and placed on the grass for safe removal by authorities.

International Heritage

Scavenging for war scrap metal in the affected areas is an entire industry. A single individual with an inexpensive store-bought metal detector and a basket on his back, such as this man (left) in Samouay District, Salavan Province, is able to collect so much saleable scrap that it begins to dwarf the floor dimensions of his house (above center). Scrap collection is often a family affair, each person with his own instrument, such as this family (above right) in Sepon District, Savannakhet Province.

Remarkably deep hand excavation of war scrap (below) at the T-intersection in the middle of Ban Dong, Sepon District, took place just before the new road cut was completed; the piece in the foreground was said to be "live."

Cluster bomb casings may be amassed by a local dealer such as this pile (right) in the Phin-Sepon District area of Savannakhet Province, and eventually consolidated into large truckloads such as the one below in the provincial town of Attapeu, headed for Vietnam.

28   Lao Close Encounters

Do the Lao bear lingering hatred toward Americans for all this? Not judging from the friendly smiles and hand gestures (above left, Vientiane) or from the occasional flag towels over porch rails (top center, Fuang District, Vientiane Province) or decals (top right, Vientiane). Senior officials and older citizens may well remember the horrors of that decade. But right now the most important consideration is the December 2004 granting of Normal Trade Relations by the U.S.A. This will enable Lao goods to enter at its lowest tariffs, including silk textiles at 0.8 percent and handicrafts at zero (Vientiane Times, 10 January 2005). Exports are expected to "soar."

An unlucky number prefix is assigned to the Embassy vehicles of a former adversary (left); is it a coincidence?

American priorities and program sponsorship in the country now include illicit drug suppression (poster, right) and corresponding infrastructure development projects; and the recovery and repatriation of the remains of American soldiers missing-in-action (MIA).

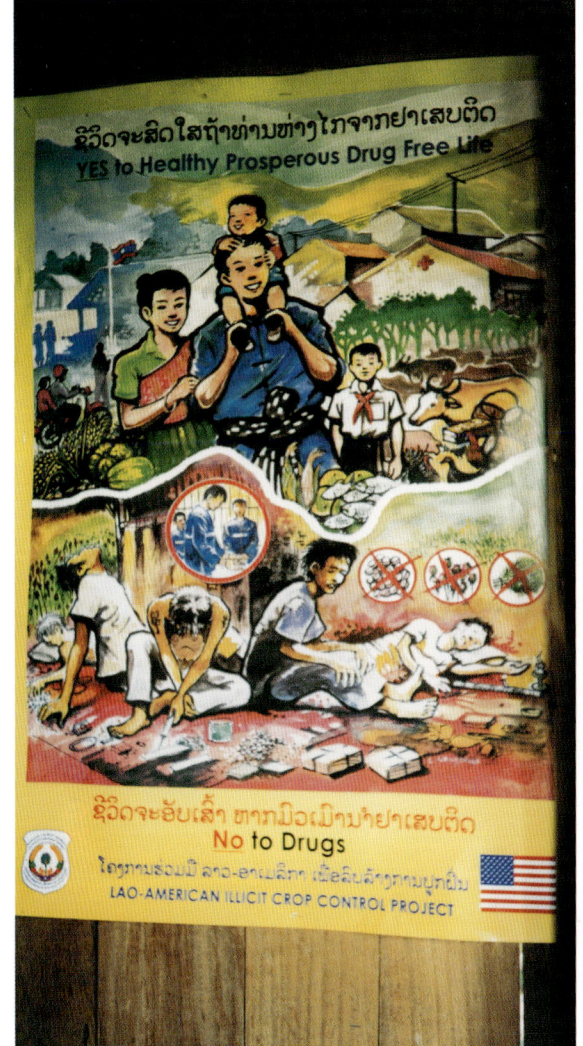

International Heritage   29

Aid Donors. Laos appreciates donor assistance from around the world, from governments and private foundations alike. Perhaps as partial atonement for its occupation of French Indochina (including Laos) during World War II, the number one aid donor is Japan. Its contribution is apparent in large infrastructure projects such as bridges and roads, the most conspicuous current project being the new Second Mekong River International Bridge between Savannakhet (signboard below left) and Mukdahan (Thailand), and also in education and in health (below right). Japan's current funding to Laos is about US$100 million per year (Vientiane Times, 6 October 2004). Japan is said to be followed in approximate order of value of development assistance by Sweden, Germany, France and Australia.

NGOs (non-governmental organizations) also find their development assistance welcomed here. Although they do not have large sums of money to work with, they are able to accomplish goals at the grassroots level in projects that are also priorities for the Lao government, including training in agriculture and public health, and in community development. A sampling of the NGOs is shown on the strips (below) from an earlier Lao government calendar. While some may have gone and others come, it is nevertheless a reasonable representation of the breadth of the helping hands. Some NGOs have been here for a long time; Quaker Service Laos, for example, has been helping out for over 30 years.

NON - GOVERNMENTAL ORGANISATIONS WORKING WITH LAO PEOPLE

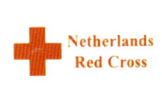

Lao Close Encounters

LIFE

Spiritual Matters. Laos is primarily a Theravada Buddhist country. Giving alms (food) to support the monks is an act of merit-making (above). You would have to get up early to see it; Vientiane.

If you visit a temple (*wat*) it is possible that a monk may approach you (above) to practice his English; Toulakhom District, Vientiane Province.

Along the road, groups of young people may approach vehicles (center left) for a contribution to temple construction or maintenance; Thapangthong District, Savannakhet Province.

Gates to temple premises may be eye-catching, such as this peacock design (left) at Viangkham District, Vientiane Province.

Buddhists have their own flag (right), used internationally; Vientiane.

Life 31

Temples are sometimes situated on an elevated plot of ground or otherwise raised from the surroundings, thus requiring stairways often with ornate balustrades. The 7-headed naga (above left) and the elephant-head entity (above right) are both at Wat Phonsan, Thaphabat District, Bolikhamsai Province. The reptilians emerging from another reptilian are in Luang Prabang (left).

Lao Close Encounters

Larger temple grounds are likely to have a 3-story tower (above left), the ground floor housing an elongate hollow wooden knocker, the *pong* (right), the middle floor with a drum, the *kong phen* (above right), stretched with buffalo hide for a very effective sound device, and the top floor with a bronze bell (left), all Vientiane.

Life 33

Regarded as the quintessential temple of the country, Wat Sieng Thong (above) stands at the tip of the Luang Prabang peninsula formed by the Mekong and Khan Rivers. Its rear façade is a tree-of-life design (right).

Luang Prabang-style temple architecture is clear in the *wat* (above) inside the grounds of the former Royal Palace.

The Luang Prabang temple style is sometimes reflected in Vientiane, such as at Wat Inpeng (below left). Contrast this with the styles of other Vientiane temples, such as (below, second to fourth left) Wat Phosai Sayalam, Wat Phiawat, and the Burmese-style Wat Si Amphon, respectively.

Lao Close Encounters

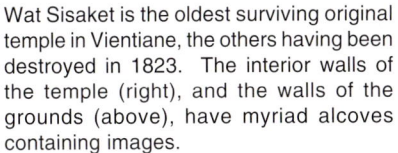

Wat Sisaket is the oldest surviving original temple in Vientiane, the others having been destroyed in 1823. The interior walls of the temple (right), and the walls of the grounds (above), have myriad alcoves containing images.

Wat Si Muang's ruins (below left) at the end of the rebuilt temple, are well bannered and protected by *nok hong* birds; the temple's interior contains the "pillar of Vientiane," only the top of which is visible above the banners (below center). By contrast, the altar of the temple in Chomphet, across the river from Luang Prabang (right), is much simpler. Modern Lao temples have ornate centerpieces called *dok so fa* on their ridgelines, such as the one on Wat Chanthabouli, Vientiane (bottom right).

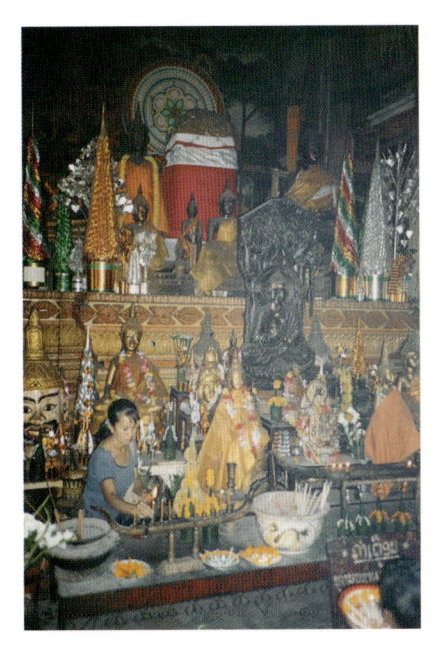

Life 35

There have been some 250,000 people from here who took refuge in the U.S.A. from 1975 onward, another part of the legacy of war. (Still more are coming in 2005 who have been in refugee camps in Thailand all this time.) Many of those new Americans have not forgotten the old country, and contribute support to relatives and temples, sometimes acknowledged right on the outer wall of the grounds (left); Hatsaifong District, Vientiane. Murals painted on the inside and outside of temple walls tell many stories, including the life of Buddha, the Ramayana, and morality.

That (pronounced as tot) is the Lao word for stupa, and for the Thai chedi. Originally to hold a relic of Buddha, it has long since been adapted for the ashes of anyone whose relatives can afford a small one. The most important and famous one in the whole country is That Luang (right) as seen through the portal of the grounds in Vientiane, commissioned by King Setthathirat. A medium sized but remarkably attractive *that* is located in the midst of rice fields in Phonhong District, Vientiane Province (below right), dedicated to a respected abbot. Smaller *that* are usually seen inside temple grounds, such as those behind Wat Haw Sin, Vientiane (below), or even incorporated into the walls of the grounds.

Lao Close Encounters

Urban temple art is incredibly ornate and photogenic from the statuary outside (*nok hong*, center right) to the doors and window shutters (above and above far right), to the main Buddha image inside (above center). When the time comes to spruce up the temple gates, a lot of red and gold paint is needed (far right). All are in Vientiane.

Life 37

Christian churches occur mostly in Mekong River towns and villages, and in other areas that were easily accessible by French missionaries. Sacred Heart Catholic Church is in Vientiane (far left), and St. Theresa Catholic Church is in Savannakhet (near left). The congregation of the Savannakhet Province church (above) traces its origin to 1888.

Hill tribes are generally spirit worshipers. The emblems on the posts (left) form a "spirit gate" guarding a village in Viangphukha District of Luang Nam Tha Province.

There is an Islamic mosque (below) in Vientiane.

Lao Close Encounters

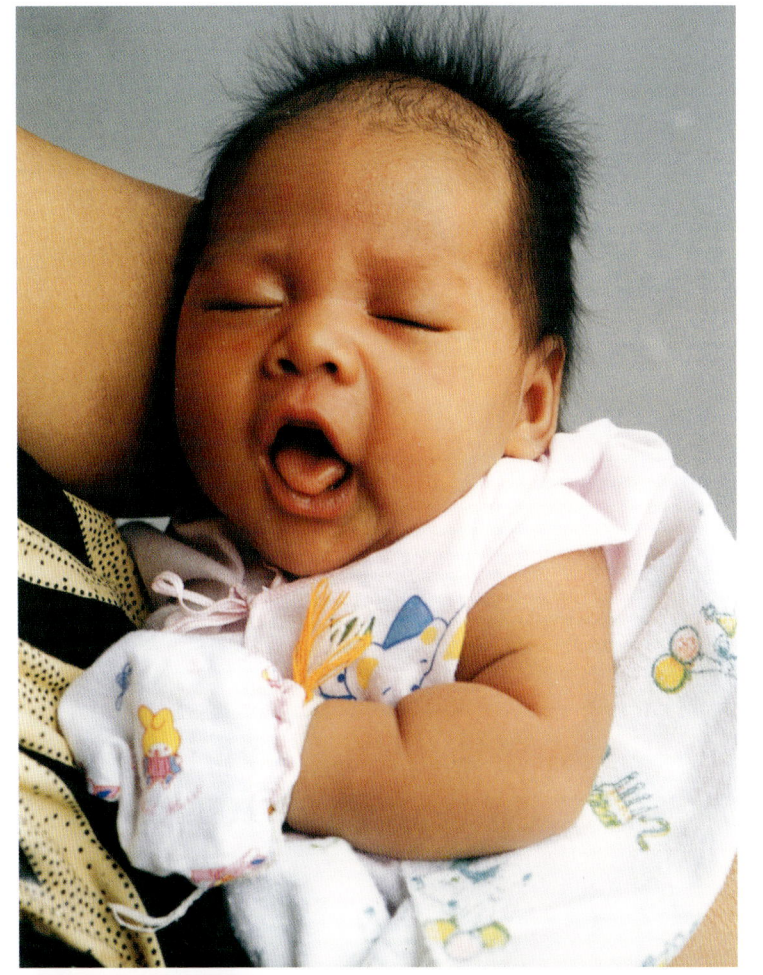

Children. Asian babies are usually born with a fairly full head of black hair; this one (left) in Vientiane is three weeks old. Not for sale: this one (above) is in a basket in the Ponsawan market, Sieng Khouang Province, but she's already spoken for.

Children always seem most in their element around water. Those seen here (below left) are swimming in the Mekong River at Pathoumphon District, opposite Champasak, and are chasing the ferry boat in the slow-flowing water. The boy (below) is also headed for the Mekong River, plunging in from a high branch in the rainy season at a temple just upstream from Vientiane.

Life

Families may enjoy the waterfalls (above) on the plateau above the western entrance to Phou Khao Khouai National Protected Area, Vientiane Province. Children deftly cross the stream on stones (above right) just above Yuang Falls in Paksong District, Champasak Province.

On the bank of the Nam Ngoum River in Thoulakhom District, Vientiane Province, a large poinciana tree has grown into the perfect shape for two young friends to share (below). In Fuang District of Vientiane Province, the kids go in for a swim right along with the tractor and cart (below right).

Lao Close Encounters

School. The teacher directs morning calisthenics at this picturesque primary school (above left) in La District, Oudomsai Province; note the footbridge over the fence, excluding wandering livestock. High school students enjoy each other's company at the end of the day in Vientiane's Hadsaifong District (above). A Vientiane teacher, apparently taking her class on a field trip, directs the students when it is safe to cross the street (left). An international school primarily for Lao students does its part to educate the younger generation in Vientiane; members of this class (below left) hold the passports of seven countries. The students of a slightly older class (below) are already taking advantage of their expanded window on the world (L. Swanson photo).

Life 41

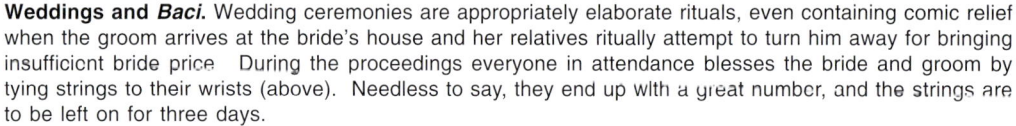

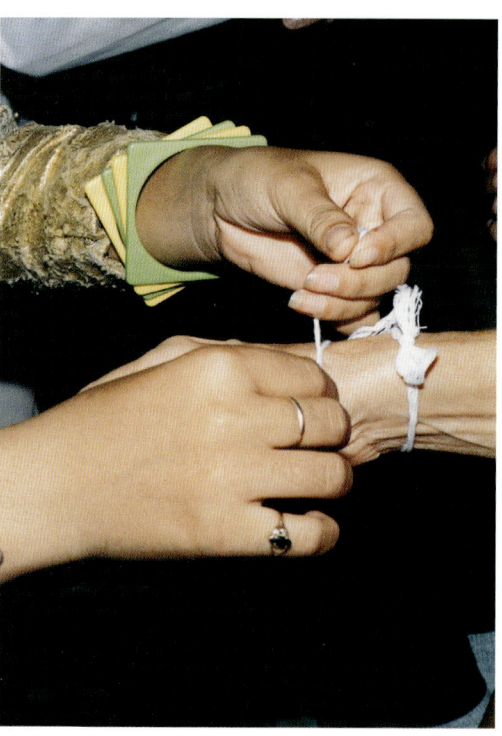

Weddings and *Baci*. Wedding ceremonies are appropriately elaborate rituals, even containing comic relief when the groom arrives at the bride's house and her relatives ritually attempt to turn him away for bringing insufficient bride price. During the proceedings everyone in attendance blesses the bride and groom by tying strings to their wrists (above). Needless to say, they end up with a great number, and the strings are to be left on for three days.

Any such ceremony with strings denoting blessings and prayers (above) is called a *baci* (pronounced *basi*) and is overseen by an elder. It takes place not only at weddings but at other milestone events including welcomes, farewells, and successes. It is of Hindu origin.

Recreation. The national favorite sport, albeit played only by males, is known internationally as sepak takraw and locally as *takaw*; watch for it any day after 4 pm. This Asian game is played with a hollow wicker or plastic ball with three on each team who kick or head the ball but do not touch it with their arms. A player executes an astute backward kick of the ball (below left) in Mounlapamok District, Champasak Province. The same game is played by military personnel on a mountaintop court (below right) along the road from Pak Mong to Luang Prabang. These players have to be rather accurate or the ball will go right over the brink.

Football (soccer) ranks high in local and national interest. This game is being played, with shoes optional, on the school grounds (left) in Khamkeut District, Bolikhamsai Province.

Volleyball ranks right up there too. This is an interprovincial game (right) between Sekong and Attapeu Provinces, being held in Attapeu town. The game is constrained to some extent because the spectators are allowed to sit right up to the lines of the court.

Games of checkers are very popular. In larger towns a concrete table can be bought with the game board molded right into it, such as the one being used by these *tuk-tuk* drivers while waiting for a fare in Vientiane (below left); but all that is really needed is a large ruled piece of paper and some bottle caps to have fun (below center) on Khong Island, Champasak Province.

And don't forget petanque, mentioned earlier, here used as an enticement to rent accommodation in a particular housing compound (below right).

Life

So far the recreational activities mentioned have not had much active participation from women. But here's one: aerobic calisthenics are catching on as an organized activity in Vientiane. Watch for it at the Chinese pavilion on Fa Ngoum Road (right) or at the corner of the fairgrounds in front of That Luang (center right).

All it takes is a little music to get the Lao to their feet to do the *lamwong*, the national dance (below right). If you approach a *lamwong* in progress, be prepared to be graciously invited to join in. These participants are creating their own extreme version (below) while humorously hamming it up for the photograph. Both are at Tat Moon Falls, Vientiane.

44   Lao Close Encounters

Just hanging out and having a picnic with friends and family at the local waterfall is seasonally popular. The Tat Moon Falls (above) is only about 17 kilometers from the center of Vientiane. The more upscale, much less crowded Hinkhanna Falls (below right) is about 25 kilometers out.

Going out for a spin on your own motorbike is a great favorite around the capital, especially if there is an errand to be run like picking up your own portrait (above left). Skateboards have just appeared recently (below).

Life 45

Showing off your prowess at cartwheels in front of an appreciative audience (above) is better than watching television any day; Vientiane.

Badminton is well regarded, and is often played on town sidewalks in addition to proper courts (above). A carnival-type game involving throwing darts to burst balloons to win small prizes has caught on recently (right); Vientiane.

Urban and rural children alike readily amuse themselves with a jump rope made from rubber bands (below), such as this group in Sieng Kho, northeastern Houa Phan Province. It is remarkable how well Lao children of mixed ages get along with each other.

Even with no equipment at all, it's fun to see which child can jump up on the back of the tolerant family buffalo in a single bound (below), in Champasak District and Province.

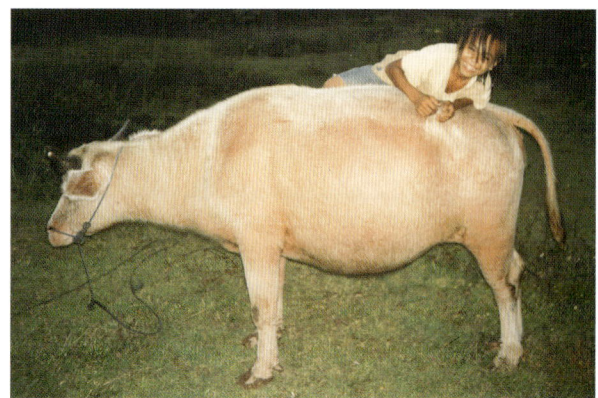

Entertainment. Passive recreation is watching someone else do the dancing (above right); or watching the Chinese opera in November (above); or having your fortune told (center left), or buying a lottery ticket (bottom left). It has been a long time indeed since the marquee of the downtown Vieng Samay theater has announced anything showing at the movies (below center), but there are now two theaters (bottom center) in the new Lao International Trade Exhibition & Convention Center (ITECC) showing movies, plus VCD and DVD rental shops all over for home viewing. One expatriate community sponsored event is the Women's International Group bazaar in November, featuring food, handicrafts, and children's activities such as choosing a model from a book and then having your face painted (below right). All Vientiane.

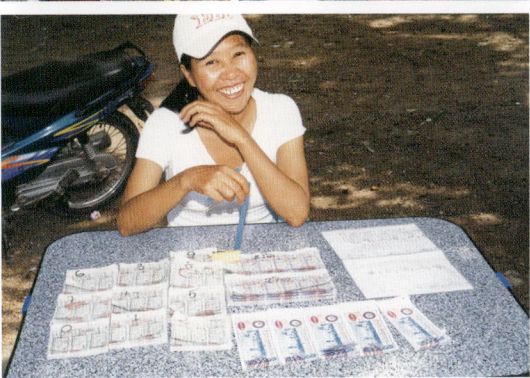

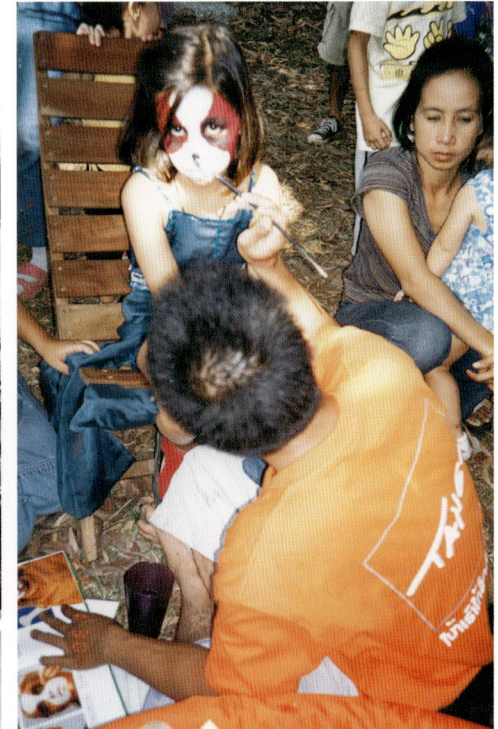

Life

Music. The *khaen* (left), that most essentially Lao instrument, plays distinctive and memorable music in the right hands. Sadly declining in popularity with the younger generation, perhaps the annual *khaen* contest, begun in 2003 at the National Cultural Hall, will breathe new life into it. An instrument maker (above) in a village just outside Luang Prabang has *saw* (with bow and strings) hanging up for sale, and is playing a xylophone-like *lanyaat*, also for sale (G.R. Ballmer photo). A drum, the *kong*, and a zither-like instrument, the *khim*, complete a Vientiane restaurant ensemble (below), while at one Luang Prabang venue the *khim* alone provides the dinner music (right).

Major ensembles may include the *khongwong*, a semicircle of horizontal gongs such as that at the right of the photo (above left), and larger drums; Luang Prabang. A walking ensemble of gong, drum, and cymbals (and beer) in Phonhong District, Vientiane Province, lacks nothing in enthusiasm (above right). Among Western instruments the guitar is surprisingly popular even in the countryside, here being played at Phou Khao Khouai National Protected Area, Vientiane Province (below left). At wedding receptions and other parties where sound equipment has been rented, invited guests are welcome to take the microphone and sing a few songs (below right), Vientiane; and the same is the case at village festivals (below center), Nasaithong, Vientiane Capital.

Life

Food. Eating sticky (glutinous) rice goes to the very essence of being Lao (above), Paksong District, Champasak Province.

One of the variants on the cooking of sticky rice is to combine it with coconut milk and then steam it in a section of bamboo, a product called "*khao lam*" (above), being sold at a festival in Vientiane.

Charcoal is plentiful, and many things are barbecued. It may be simple sausages and potatoes on skewers at roadside (below) in Vientiane; or it may be an onslaught of barbecued chicken (*kai ping*) offered up to bus stop passengers (near right) in Pak Kading District, Bolikhamsai Province. The sheer volume of chicken (far right) available to festival revelers in Vientiane is remarkable.

50   Lao Close Encounters

Tilapia, locally called *pa nil* which accurately reflects the Nile origins of this locally farmed fish, is barbecued with an outer encrustation of salt (above left). Most barbecues involve small sized animals, but here is an entire calf (above) being roasted at the end of Buddhist lent in Vientiane.

Often done but not often seen, the Vietnamese community relishes the purported vitamins available from barbecued canines (left), Kham District, Sieng Khouang Province.

This may not be widely available, but here is a vegetarian's delight of barbecued vegetables (below left) in Vientiane. Deep frying is also done, as with this stack of doughnuts available for sale in Luang Prabang (below), while the proprietress prepares more dough.

Life

Insect eating is common; at a forest gatherers' market at Mahasai cave, Khammouan Province, ant pupae and adults are offered (top left). Even in Vientiane, children consider it worthwhile to tap leaf clusters in a vacant lot with a long bamboo pole and a plastic bag (above), hoping that ant pupae will drop in from any nest. Insect eating also extends to beetles and to giant water bugs, *maeng da*, (below), offered at Ponsawan market, Sieng Khouang Province.

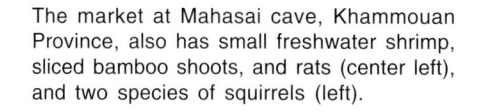

The market at Mahasai cave, Khammouan Province, also has small freshwater shrimp, sliced bamboo shoots, and rats (center left), and two species of squirrels (left).

Lao Close Encounters

Restaurant food: a decent breakfast may consist of a bowl of Vietnamese-style noodle soup (called *foe*, *feu*, *fur* or *pho*, whichever transliteration you prefer), the ubiquitous dish of the whole country (left), usually served with a large dish of raw greens; if you think they would be more sanitary if cooked in the soup, the shopkeeper might (or might not) be willing to put some types of greens in for you, as shown here. This set is rounded out with baguette and jam, and tea; Luang Prabang.

A tasty lunch for two could be a whole fried Tilapia fish smothered in sweet-and-sour style vegetables, a plate of pork with ginger, and plates of rice (below); Phonhong District, Vientiane Province.

A good dinner for two might be green curry with chicken, sautéed mixed vegetables, and sticky rice, the latter shown here as a mixture of white and dark-grained varieties (above); Luang Prabang. Shared dishes do not usually come to the table with serving spoons, as the Lao eat with, and serve themselves with, the same spoon. If you want separate serving spoons, just ask.

Life

Festivals. Twelve of these occur at various times throughout the year, some of which are long-awaited. Even the smaller festivals are celebrated in the villages with a money tree dance procession to the temple to make merit. This one (below) may be *Boun Phawed San Don*, early in the year.

Pi Mai Lao, Lao New Year, is in April. It is celebrated in various ways, the most conspicuous of which is "blessing" one another with water. It is quite remarkable how excellent one's aim with a bowl of water can become with a little practice (above right).

This blessing began as a polite pouring of water over the shoulder, but has evolved into something of a public free-for-all. Tuk-tuk passengers are "sitting ducks" and receive a total drenching (center right), while a truck with water-throwing passengers may receive massive retaliation from both sides of the road (right). Dye is sometimes added to the water, as seen on this well-blessed truck (above). This festival is in the middle of the dry season, so authorities try to stop it in order to conserve scarce water resources, but apparently to no avail. Needless to say it's fun but poses additional risk to cyclists. All Vientiane Capital.

A large number of Lao youth convene (above) at Tat Lo Falls, Laongam District, Salavan Province, all soaking wet from having thoroughly "blessed" each other for New Year.

Here comes a village contingent of dancing, *khaen*-playing *Pi Mai* revelers right down Route 13S (left) in southern Savannakhet Province. There are some dye-stained hands indicating earlier merriment among this truckload of young revelers (below) in Champhon District, Savannakhet Province, yet water is so scarce in the dry season that there is only one remaining water shooter in sight with which to celebrate.

Life

Boun Bang Fai, the Rocket Festival, is in May. The purpose of this one is to alert the powers above that it is time to start the rainy season so that the rice fields can be prepared. A rocket takes a proud turn through Vientiane (top left) before heading out to the launch pad. Well-decorated rockets are carried into the temple grounds adjacent to the launch site (top right and center left); once inside, female elders (above) do their part to see that the rockets deliver their message; when the time comes, the rockets are undressed and carried to the launch pad, and here the "business end" of a rocket is exposed (left); all Nasaithong, Vientiane Capital.

Lao Close Encounters

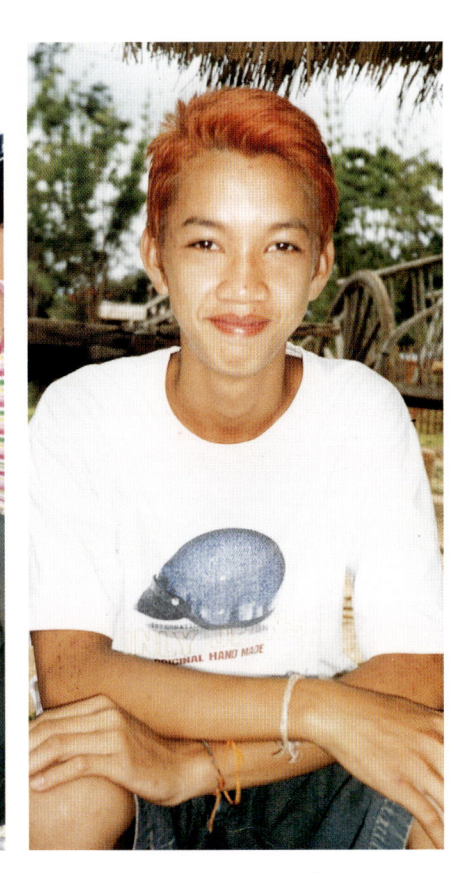

A rocket soars skyward in a successful launch; surprisingly, the launchers stay right up on the pad throughout the process (above left). The whole event is highly competitive, with prizes for the best flights. The somewhat phallic nature of the event is not lost on this woman (above center), who is toting around a 2-meter "log" amongst the celebrants. Such events may be the time to try out a new fashion, such as dyed hair (above right); all Nasaithong, Vientiane Capital. The Rocket Festival is not confined to the Vientiane area by any means; here is a used launch pad (below left) in Sing District, Luang Nam Tha Province. A periodic ceremony: the faithful follow the monks three times around the *that* (below), here taking place atop the hill overlooking the town of Oudomsai.

Life

October sees another village procession to the temple (above left), as it is the festival commemorating the end of Buddhist Lent, *Awk Phansaa*, also known as the boat racing festival. This is a very social occasion, with hopeful vendors setting up additional food and clothing stalls (above center), and entertainment such as the ferris wheel (above right) is added; all Vientiane and vicinity. This is also the time when the *lai heua fai* ceremony takes place, when Buddhists construct small floats of bamboo and banana tree cross sections and decorate them with flowers, candles, and incense sticks. If a stream is nearby, the floats are launched into it; if not, they are lighted at the temple. The symbolism of the event has various interpretations. Young folks enjoy preparing their *lai heua fai* (left) and launching them down the river at Vang Vieng, Vientiane Province. Remarkable long boats, stored at the temple for the rest of the year (below left), will be shaped up and made ready in time for the races; Viangkham District, Vientiane Province. In Luang Prabang, this entire boat has been turned into a gigantic *lai heua fai* (below), commemorating the Naga of the Mekong River.

58   Lao Close Encounters

The That Luang Festival in late November is the largest Vientiane-centered event of the year, taking place over several days, and attracting monks (left) and ordinary folks alike from all over the country. Local vendors such as the balloon sales boy (right) hope to turn a profit from the festive mood of the crowd.

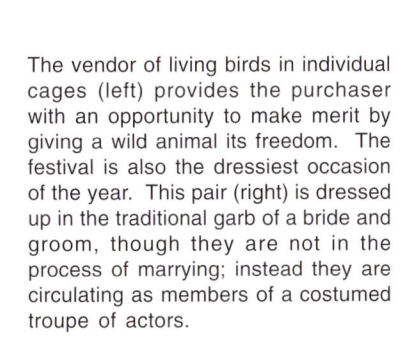

The vendor of living birds in individual cages (left) provides the purchaser with an opportunity to make merit by giving a wild animal its freedom. The festival is also the dressiest occasion of the year. This pair (right) is dressed up in the traditional garb of a bride and groom, though they are not in the process of marrying; instead they are circulating as members of a costumed troupe of actors.

Life

On the big day, the monks arrive and assume their places early in the morning (top left). Buddhist nuns are also represented, but their numbers are low (above). Eventually, the general population files through the gate (center left). In due time, the entire enormous courtyard fills (bottom left), and the faithful wait patiently, alms offerings before them, for instructions (below).

Lao Close Encounters

On signal, all *nop* in unison as a sign of respect (above left), followed by the symbolic raising of alms bowls (above right).

Later, all rise and the faithful move up and down the rows of monks, giving a little to each as long as their supply lasts, all under the watch of the statue of King Setthathirat.

Life 61

Tribal Life. There are over a hundred ethnic groups in the country, an astounding diversity kept heterogeneous by montane isolation. On the other hand, for various reasons many groups have succumbed to assimilation in dress and have adopted Lao or Western clothing thereby making themselves relatively indistinguishable from majority populations. This is a disappointment that is best overcome by going to more remote areas to the north and northwest of Luang Prabang, especially to Luang Nam Tha and Phongsali Provinces, where traditional attire is much more likely still to be seen.

As a case in point, the woman (left) lives in Paksong District in the central Boloven Plateau and it is a reasonable assumption that she is of the Loven group, but how would we know? The man (upper left) lives in Sieng Ngeun District of Luang Prabang Province and continues to wear standard Hmong tribal clothing. The man (upper right) lives in Phoukhoun District of Luang Prabang and is also tribal but has Western dress; a small percentage of tribal youngsters have pale hair. The three girls (above) live in Khamkeut District of Bolikhamsai Province, and are sporting the most exquisite Hmong clothing, which would only be worn at the most important of ceremonies. Tribal women are of necessity very hard working, but despite their burdens, these ladies (right) in Phoukhoun District still manage smiles for passing tourists.

Lao Close Encounters

Tribal settlement patterns are variable, but one that is often seen in the northern mountains is the road shoulder village. Taking advantage of what may be the only flat ground around, and also the proximity of transportation, a village may be strung out along the narrow road shoulder in a single line of houses such as the one (above left) in Phongsali Province, or may occupy both sides of the road such as the one (above right) in Luang Prabang Province. It is a precarious existence with potential danger from speeding vehicles just outside the front door, and a precipice at the rear. Depending on the availability of flatter ground and a water source, tribal villages of more ordinary dimensions may also be seen, such as the one (below left) across the stream in Sienghon/Ngeun District, Sayabouli Province. Some villages may have ornate spirit gates, perhaps at both entrances, such as those (below center and right) in Sing District, Luang Nam Tha Province.

Life

With its desirable position, this village house (above) doubles as a roadside stand; human life expectancy may not be high in the hills, but having a lot of children compensates for it (above right); basic yet ingenious mechanical advantage devices are used extensively, such as this grinder turning cassava into a slurry for cooking (right); all in Phoukhoun District, Luang Prabang Province.

Variation on the theme: these women are grinding corn for animal feed (left) in Khoun District, Sieng Khouang Province.

Lao Close Encounters

Water is truly precious in the hills. Clever villagers may be able to tap into a small seepage in a rock crevice and "pipe" it to the road, sometimes over a considerable distance, by hollowing out bamboo stems (left) as seen here in Khop/Sienghon District, Sayabouli Province. Such a tap is drinking, cooking, bathing and washing water for the village (above), as well as a great convenience for passersby; Phoukhoun District, Luang Prabang Province. Villages on mountaintops such as the one (below left) in eastern Phoukhoun District have a major problem procuring water in the dry season.
Hard-won mountain crops must be protected from post-harvest losses; one of the most important ways is to put rodent proof barriers on the legs of the granaries (right), as in Viangphukha District, Luang Nam Tha Province.

If you want to settle for the stylized version of tribal life, it can be seen at a performance in Vientiane (below right).

Life 65

Death. In some traditions, it is appropriate to hold a viewing so that friends may bid their final farewell to the deceased (above left); a single-file procession, with each participant holding onto a rope that is attached to the coffin on the truck at the rear (above right) progresses to the place where the cremation is to be held; Vientiane.

Below, the coffin has been placed atop a stand in a rural memorial ground, while a service is held by the monks and attended by female family members dressed in white; piles of sticks are ignited so that each participant may contribute to the pyre; and the flames do their work (right), with ashes eventually to be placed in a commemorative *that*; Hin Hoep District, Vientiane Province.

AGRICULTURE AND FORESTRY

Rice Is Life Is Rice. Laos is an agrarian society, and above all agricultural pursuits is the cultivation of rice. After the onset of the rainy season has turned the fields to mud, it is time to plow. This is mostly done with a water buffalo, but in more affluent areas the "iron buffalo" (above) is making inroads; Nasaithong District, Vientiane Capital. In the meantime, well-defended rice nurseries grow the seedlings; when the right time comes, the seedlings are bundled for transportation to the main fields (above right); Khamkeut District, Bolikhamsai Province. Transplanting the rice seedlings is very much a group effort (below), with extended family members who may have other jobs returning "home" to participate; Houai Sai District, Bokeo Province. Transplantation is done in a very difficult posture, and some senior citizens who have done it for many years may no longer be able to stand fully straight again (below right); Vang Vieng District, Vientiane Province (G.R. Ballmer photo).

Agriculture and Forestry 67

After the rice has been set out (top left), the two most important jobs remaining are to maintain proper water balance, and to defend the fields against hungry herbivores; Khamkeut District, Bolikhamsai Province. Glutinous ("sticky") rice, preferred by the Lao, is commonly grown on hillsides (top right); Bokeo Province. Ripening rice heads are so heavy that they droop under the weight of the crop (center left); Khamkeut District. While the great majority of rice is white, some dark varieties are also grown, with their color obvious even in the field (above); Soukhouma District, Champasak Province. A ripe rice field is truly a glorious sight to behold (left); Met/Kasi District, Vientiane Province.

Lao Close Encounters

When harvest time arrives, family groups assemble again (especially the women) and use their sickles to turn the stalks into tied sheaths (top left); Met District, Vientiane Province. Gradually the stalks fall to the knife (top right) until the job is completed; Hin Boun District, Khammouan Province. There follows a drying period. This may be accomplished in various ways, the most artistic of which is the stack method (center left) seen in western Sieng Khouang Province and neighboring areas. Usually the sheaves are dried on racks in or near the fields, and can be transported "home" later (center right); Champasak District and Province. Small sheaves, such as these heads of sticky rice (right) may simply be splayed out on a table or other dry surface; Khamkeut District, Bolikhamsai Province.

Agriculture and Forestry

Now comes the requirement for separating the rice heads from the straw. In its most elementary form, this can be accomplished by whacking the sheaves on a tarpaulin in the field, then doing an initial winnowing to remove chaff without kernels (top left); Phoun District, Saisomboun Special Zone. The job of separating rice heads from sheaves is made so much easier by an ingenious foot-powered device that even a young girl can manage single-handedly (above); Champasak District and Province. The modern alternative is to bring in machine-powered equipment into which rice stems are fed, which then forcibly ejects the straw and directs the rice into a waiting bag (left); Pek District, Sieng Khouang Province. Now it is on to the next step: separating the rice kernels from their chaff coat. Once again, there are degrees of sophistication in this process. Pounding the chaff off the kernels with the use of a kind of mallet, often done by two women in alternating strikes (bottom left), is commonly seen; Saibouathong District, Khammouan Province. A clever labor-saving alternative, seen only once in Sienghon District, Sayabouli Province, is to use the weight of running water to raise and then lower a balanced bar in order to pound the grain (below).

70 Lao Close Encounters

A truck-mounted rice mill may be driven right into a village to accomplish the separation (above left); Pathoumphon District, Champasak Province. Or farmers may transport their grain to a permanent rice mill with heavier-duty machinery (above center and above right); at the rear of the mill, chickens pick through the fresh blown chaff looking for kernels (center left); Champhon District, Savannakhet Province. Even after all this, it helps to clean the kernels again with one final winnowing before cooking (right); Viangthong DIstrict, Houa Phan Province. Here, the finished product is an appetizing basket of mixed variety sticky rice (below left) as served in a restaurant in Luang Prabang.

Agriculture and Forestry

71

Fish Farming and Fishing. Aquaculture is practiced in several ways, including netted holding pens in the Mekong River such as these (above left) in Hatsaifong District, Vientiane Capital, where the owner is seen feeding his carp. Much more common is the farm pond in which Tilapia (*pa nil*, reflecting their origin in the Nile) are successfully grown; most of the fish in the aquarium (above right) are Tilapia; Keo-Oudom District, Vientiane Province. Another technique is to scoop all the water from one side of a dike to the other (center right) in order to catch every last minnow as the wet season wanes (Khamkeut District, Bolikhamsai Province). Another is to dragnet a body of water such as a borrow pit (below right); Champasak Province. Throw netting is a picturesque method (below); Nasaithong District, Vientiane Capital. New throw nets are being prepared for use (left); Khong District, Champasak Province.

Lao Close Encounters

With the Mekong River at low stage, a fisherman tries some drift netting from his boat (above left); Vientiane sandbar. Barely able to keep his foothold in the torrent, a fisherman works his net in the small ebb of a cascade below a dam (above right) on the Nam Et River, Et District, Houa Phan Province. His effort pays off handsomely (center right).

Lift netting is done in slow flowing water such as the canal between flooded rice fields (center left) lined with villagers. On signal, all of them yank up their nets in unison (below left) to maximize the catch; Phonhong District, Vientiane Province.

Fish trapping is done where a strong current is narrowly channeled. Here, one of the Mekong River gorges cutting across Don Khone Island (lower right) has a fish trap; Khong District, Champasak Province.

Agriculture and Forestry

Ladies return home (above left) with some of the bounty of the Nam Thoen River; Khamkeut District, Bolikhamsai Province. Judging from the paraphernalia they are carrying, these intent young villagers (top right) are all going fishing together; Viangsai District, Houa Phan Province.   Two boys (below left) on the bank of the Mekong River at the southern end of Don Chan Island practice their lift netting technique; Vientiane. A fish vendor at a ferry crossing on the Mekong River tends the catch in her holding cages (center right), Pathoumphon District; this is one species (below center) that forms part of the varied catch for sale at the Pakse city market; and a dried fish vendor at Veunkham, the last village before the Cambodian border, is ready to sell his stock (below right), Khong District; all Champasak Province. The greater Mekong River Basin is said to be among those with the highest fish species diversity in the world, but hydroelectric development on the Mekong and on its tributaries alike is bound to have a deleterious effect.

74   Lao Close Encounters

Vegetables. There never seems to be any lack of fresh produce. A farmer tends her plots (far left) in March directly in the path of what has historically been a flood stage channel of the Mekong River in August. On the iron footbridge above her, another farmer pushes a cartload of newly harvested kale crops (near left) out to the main road where she will sell directly to the public. Alternatively, wholesalers may go straight to the farm and buy a crop no sooner than it has been pulled out of the ground (below left), in this case a harvest of the yam bean, *mun pao*. All Don Chan Island, Vientiane.

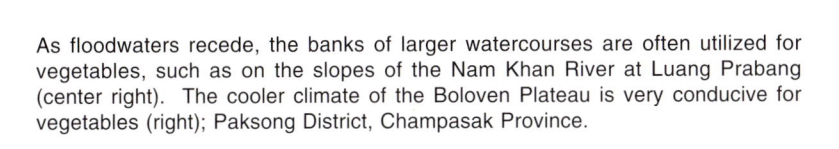

As floodwaters recede, the banks of larger watercourses are often utilized for vegetables, such as on the slopes of the Nam Khan River at Luang Prabang (center right). The cooler climate of the Boloven Plateau is very conducive for vegetables (right); Paksong District, Champasak Province.

Agriculture and Forestry

75

City vegetable markets show a remarkable array of colors (above left and above center); it would be difficult to count the number of vegetable species for sale here; Vientiane. This vendor at the Pakse city new market (left) specializes in items that impart flavor; Champasak Province. While there is no longer much demand, this vendor (above right) is selling betel nut; Soukhouma District, Champasak Province. Sugar cane is for sale by roadside (right) in Bolikhamsai Province.

Drying space for grain always seems to be at a premium. Corn, mostly for animal feed, can be dried right on the road (below right), or can be festooned in a proud manner around the house (below left); Namo and Houn Districts, Oudomsai Province.

Lao Close Encounters

Another field crop, with a growth form quite similar to corn but without the ears, is called Job's tears (*mak leuay*) (far left); it has a bland taste but is combined with flavorful ingredients to make desserts; Viangthong District, Houa Phan Province. Cassava grows easily (near left); its roots make tapioca, another dessert product (Vientiane Capital).

Sesame seed production is a curious process. The mature plant (right) has pods growing upright from the leaf axils, which when ripe open at the top of the pods. The stalks are carefully cut with a knife, tied in bundles and then firmly reattached vertically to the still-rooted stalk bases to dry (below left), so that the seeds do not fall out. The farmer then comes by with a basket and taps the seeds into it (below center). This process is repeated over a period of time until the farmer is satisfied that the seeds have mostly all fallen out. The chaff is then removed and the small but precious harvest is complete (below right). Ngoi District, Luang Prabang Province.

Agriculture and Forestry

The theme of drying space at a premium plays out over and over. Red chillies may be dried on a tarpaulin on the road (above left), as in Kasi District, Vientiane Province, or more efficiently by creating a layered effect (above), as in Kham District, Sieng Khouang Province.

Grandmother and grandson see to the drying peanut crop (below) in La District, Oudomsai Province.

There is a bumper crop of red bell peppers (capsicum) (center) in Boun Neua District, and even though this is one of the most important road intersections (Route 1 with Route 19 to the China border) in all of Phongsali Province, the traffic circle itself (above) is the best space available to dry more peppers.

Lao Close Encounters

Fruit. Urban Lao fruit markets (above left) contain not only local produce but also more temperate zone items like apples and pears imported from neighboring China and year-round tropical items imported from neighboring Thailand; this stand includes mangosteens, longkong, several grape varieties, lychees, mangoes, several citrus varieties, melons, and coconuts; Vientiane. Roadside stands are a welcome sight for travelers (above), even if the offered items (bananas and papayas) all seem to be the same color. Just stop your vehicle and the roadside produce may come to you (center left): children compete with one another for the traveler's business by dangling their bananas in the window; Bachiangcharoensouk District, Champasak Province.

Truckloads of tasty watermelons (bottom left) are unloaded by roadside for quick sale during a seasonal glut in November; Vientiane. Value added: vendors with carts make it easy to buy fruit snacks (below), here with jujubes, mangoes, pomelo, and sugar cane; Thoulakhom District, Vientiane Province.

Agriculture and Forestry

More roadside vendor service with a smile: longan fruits are bagged (below); and a cartload of rambutans are proudly displayed (near right); Vientiane. Lotus heads (far right) with their bitter seeds are plentiful; Vientiane.

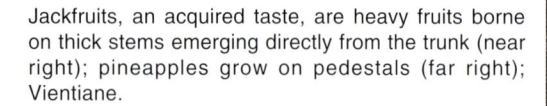

Jackfruits, an acquired taste, are heavy fruits borne on thick stems emerging directly from the trunk (near right); pineapples grow on pedestals (far right); Vientiane.

Lao Close Encounters

Mangoes drape from the trees in April like ornaments (above left); starfruit (carambola) may be so plentiful on a single tree (above right) that the farmer does not bother to take them to market, and instead the passerby may help himself; Vientiane. Some fruit such as *mak lawt* (below left) is known by the Lao to be edible in modest quantities, but it is not seen in the market; Vang Vieng District, Vientiane Province.

Poppies. While opium poppies have been a major cash crop in the past, the government is quite serious about eliminating it, and currently targets 2005 to be the end of cultivation, while acknowledging rehabilitation of addicts will take longer (Vientiane Times 10 December 2004). Positive statistics about cultivation eradication or reduction on the provincial and district levels have appeared regularly in the press. Indeed, unless you go out on a purposeful guided trek to find them, it is highly unlikely that you will see any poppies at all. Dried pods (for seed?) were once seen for sale in a Ponsawan market (right); Pek District, Sieng Khouang Province.

Agriculture and Forestry

Domestic Animals. There are two ways to see that herbivorous animals do not eat the crops: either tether the animals so that they do not have access to the fields before harvest; or fence the fields so that the animals may run loose. Laos clearly has a preference for the latter. Loose cattle (above) "clutter" the road in Vang Vieng District, Vientiane Province. Fenced fields (above right) are shown here in Pek District, Sieng Khouang Province. Cattle (center right), like crops, seem to do especially well in the cooler weather of the Boloven Plateau; Champasak Province.

While losing out steadily to the "iron buffalo," the real water buffalo (below) is a hard-working, typically non-aggressive beast that has been on duty in rice paddies, and even in a few dry fields, for centuries without requiring any petrol; Don Chan, Vientiane. Small horses are widely used as pack animals in the mountains and other remote areas; Samouay District, Salavan Province.

Lao Close Encounters

Goats are clearly the most agile members of the domestic lineup, and sometimes they succeed in being comedians, such as when they appear to be ants poking out the top of a giant anthill (below); Khamkeut District, Bolikhamsai Province. Goats are self-disciplined on the roadways for they often walk in a tight column along the road shoulder out of danger, though on a narrow bridge (below) they may appear to be taking up more than their share of space; Hin Boun District, Khammouan Province.

In "The Land of a Million Elephants" (*Lan Sang, Lane Xang*), it is still a reasonable expectation that in some parts of the country the traveler may yet encounter working elephants along the road (top left); Tha Phabat District, Bolikhamsai Province. Elephants need work breaks too, and village children are quick to take advantage of the recreational opportunity in a passing pachyderm (above), even to the extent of going swimming with it (center); Pakse District, Champasak Province.

Agriculture and Forestry

83

Pot bellied, sway-backed swine are the mainstay of mountain and lowland villages alike. With the abdomen actually scraping the ground at full pregnancy (above left), this prolific animal is an efficient converter of feed to meat; Khoun District, Sieng Khouang Province. A soft bed of leaves serves this on-demand mother well; Vilabouli District, Savannakhet Province.

Dogs are widely kept. When whole groups of them are led on ropes through a village (below), it can be surmised that they are destined to be more than just pets; Nam Bak District, Luang Prabang Province. Rabbit raising (below right) is not often seen; Kenthao District, Sayabouli Province.

Lao Close Encounters

Whoever coined the phrase "goose stepping" to describe a particular marching style knew his geese: like choreographed performers leaving the adjoining school, the geese proceed in unison (above) in Bolikhamsai Province. A duck rearing operation (below) is successful in Vientiane Province, but as a result of persistent outbreaks of avian (bird) flu in various Southeast Asian countries, free range duck farming like this may not continue indefinitely, as the problem may put Lao farmers under pressure to confine the birds for less exposure and closer monitoring. A chicken oversees her large family (center left) in Sayabouli Province. Feathers fly in a spontaneous cockfight between two rivals (upper left) near Luang Prabang.

A drake takes a break (below) outside Luang Prabang; and tom turkeys try to impress the hens (below right) in Sieng Khouang Province.

Agriculture and Forestry

Silviculture. Growing tree crops is a relatively recent concept in the country. The only two kinds that have been planted widely are teak and eucalyptus. Several others are in their infancy but may be developed quickly. Teak is native and was once an important forest tree species, but has long since been cut. Teak plantations can be seen throughout the country as a means of reforestation on a private scale, as it is relatively fast growing and desirable. It is planted in dense rows to make the trees grow tall and straight, and is readily identifiable along the roadside by its large leaves (above left); Phonsai District, Luang Prabang Province; and slightly older (right); Bachiangcharoensouk District, Champasak Province.

Eucalyptus is native of Australia, is wonderfully fast growing and is used for furniture and paper products. It is also planted in tight rows (right); Hin Boun District, Khammouan Province. Some rubber has been grown on a very limited scale, such as this plantation (left) outside of Pakse, Champasak Province; but this industry is apparently on the verge of a rapid expansion here, with Chinese companies investing in Oudomsai and Phongsali Provinces, and other countries investing farther south. Expensive agar wood, *Aquilaria*, highly prized in the Middle East as a fragrance, is planted in a few places in Saisomboun Special Zone, Sieng Khouang and Bolikhamsai Provinces.

The Forest. The Lao forest is truly the heritage of their future generations. It is under tremendous pressure from the requirements of a very rapidly expanding population. Previously, large families were encouraged on the theory that this would promote development, but it has since been realized that it is to the benefit of all to have a balance between population growth and resources. Only recently have government officials begun publicly to express concern over the negative impact that the high fertility rate will have on economic development (Vientiane Times, 14 July & 9 November 2004). Nevertheless, the Lao forest is still more extensive than that of some of its neighbors, perhaps due in part to its relative inaccessibility and to loss of population from war and emigration of refugees. According to statistics provided by the Forestry Department Head as quoted in the Vientiane Times of 25 February 2004, in 1940 Laos was 70% forested, by 1992 it was down to 47%; no current figure was given but clearly the forest is disappearing fast. The idea, of course, is to have the forest be a sustainable resource which can support the economic requirements of the country indefinitely while at the same time conserve water and sustain its heritage as a truly outstanding reservoir of biodiversity of life forms. Toward this latter goal, the government has wisely established a series of National Biodiversity and Conservation Areas, currently abbreviated to National Protected Areas, though these are not well defended against encroachment.

A bulldozer track delimits the path of the relocated Route 18 through Sansai District, Attapeu Province to the Vietnam border (top left), through some fine forest of the Dong Amphan National Protected Area. Another forest view, this time along the road from Sienghon to Ngeun District, Sayabouli Province (top right); villagers taking a tree to build a house means almost nothing to the overall scheme of things. Seeds from dipterocarp trees spin to the earth (left) in Sanamsai District, Attapeu Province; this tree family is one of the forest dominants.

Agriculture and Forestry

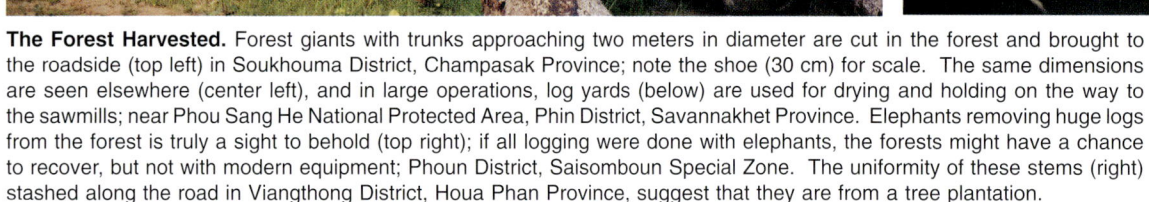

The Forest Harvested. Forest giants with trunks approaching two meters in diameter are cut in the forest and brought to the roadside (top left) in Soukhouma District, Champasak Province; note the shoe (30 cm) for scale. The same dimensions are seen elsewhere (center left), and in large operations, log yards (below) are used for drying and holding on the way to the sawmills; near Phou Sang He National Protected Area, Phin District, Savannakhet Province. Elephants removing huge logs from the forest is truly a sight to behold (top right); if all logging were done with elephants, the forests might have a chance to recover, but not with modern equipment; Phoun District, Saisomboun Special Zone. The uniformity of these stems (right) stashed along the road in Viangthong District, Houa Phan Province, suggest that they are from a tree plantation.

Post-Harvest Losses. Logs left by roadside to dry or to await their turn at the sawmill, if not retrieved in a timely fashion, may suffer a variety of fates that are deplorable by any standard. They may be lost to fungal rot, termites and other insect damage (top left). Or they may burn down to a useless charred waste when villagers (who are unrelated to the logging procedure) set fire to clear brush in the general vicinity (top and center right); all Mounlapamok District, Champasak Province. Such losses are so easily avoidable by only cutting down what can be properly processed.

The gathering of resin (used for various things including waterproofing of boats) is done in a remarkably wasteful way (left) that ultimately kills and even burns down large trees, such as in Pathoumphon District, Champasak Province. Another kind of burning, this time economically necessary: the making of charcoal for cooking utilizes sticks as shown (right); Khanthabouli District, Savannakhet Province.

Agriculture and Forestry

Slash-and-Burn. The extravagance of gaining soil fertility for crops by burning down the forest is one that the country can ill afford. Tropical soils are fragile, especially on slopes, and the repetition of burn cycles provides ever less return. The government has long been concerned about this, e.g. note the 1989 postage stamp (below left), but the practice persists. The government poverty reduction program involves relocating these mountain farmers down to the lowlands to practice permanent cultivation, now with specific guidelines for provincial authorities; we can hope that the displacement is done in a way that is least destructive to ethnic societies, with appropriate services provided, and with facilitation of entry into the larger market economy. The forest is torched (above left) in Phoun District, Saisomboun Special Zone; visibility is impaired for driving, and breathing is not so easy either (above right) in Kasi District, Vientiane Province. Whole hillsides are consumed at a time (left), here seen near the Vientiane/Luang Prabang Province border (note the northbound bus); when it is over, the only things still smoking are the larger tree trunks (below), in the same general area. Most of the burning takes place in March and April.

The sheer ugliness of the aftermath of slash-and-burn where once a proud forest stood is a remarkable sight. Sadly, slash-and-burn is not limited to the mountains (above left), Mounlapamok District, Champasak Province, and (right) Dong Amphan National Protected Area, Sansai District, Attapeu Province. Just as in the pioneering days of America when "the good burn" freed up space for more pasture, it does not seem to matter how much area is burned off. The first order of business after the burn is to put up a field shack (left); Longsan/Hom District, Vientiane Province. In an area repeatedly slashed-and-burned, several degrees of regeneration may be seen (below left); Luang Prabang/Oudomsai Province border area. The patina of the new crop covers the hills (below right) in northern Luang Prabang Province. Reforestation on a large scale is in its infancy.

Agriculture and Forestry

OTHER INTERESTING OCCUPATIONS

Mulberries. These are small trees that are kept pruned as bushes (above left), and are grown for their berries and their leaves. The berries are harvested ripe and are then prepared (above right) as food, which may be in the form of fruit shakes (center left) that can be sipped while eating a fruit pancake with honey, or the berries could also be added into the pancake. They may also be used to make wine. The leaves may be made into tea, or may be chopped to feed to silkworms (below left). These in turn pupate, and their cocoons are turned into spun silk (below). All of this may be seen, and consumed, at an organic farm under the capable ownership of this fascinating man (right), just a few kilometers north of the town of Vang Vieng, Vientiane Province.

92 Lao Close Encounters

Mulberry Paper. This remarkable industry can be observed in some northern provinces, and there is high demand for the product. The scientific name of the paper mulberry is *Broussonetia papyrifera,* and it is not the same genus or species as the edible mulberry (*Morus*) though it is in the same family. It is native to Laos, has the local name *posa*, and is now also grown in private plantations. In March, the branches are stripped of their bark. Sometimes it is a long walk home with a heavy load (right) from the place of the harvest; Phiang District, Sayabouli Province. The inner bark is then hung up to dry around the village (center left); Pak Lai District, Sayabouli Province.

There follows a great deal of boiling and pounding (below left) until the product is turned into a "mash," as seen outside Luang Prabang. This slurry is then applied to a drying rack, drained, and the rack is placed out to dry (below); outside Luang Nam Tha. The dry paper is later peeled off the rack.

Other Interesting Occupations

In a higher degree of sophistication, the slurry is prepared in a screened frame and bits of fern, grass, flower bracts or petals are added (above left and above right); and coloring may also be added (center left); the resulting paper may have frames added and then be cut (center right), until ultimately lanterns and other products result (below left); all in villages just upriver from Luang Prabang. These products are also for sale in the Luang Prabang night market, many of them thoughtfully collapsible for the tourist's suitcase (below right). Sheets of the product can also be bought as gift wrapping paper.

Lao Close Encounters

The export potential of mulberry paper has been recognized, and a Thai joint venture company is turning it into something more than just a cottage industry. Processing plants are being set up in Sayabouli Province; bundles of the raw product are being collected in Phiang District (above).

A handicraft development association (above right) near the Nam Ngoum Reservoir south of Vang Vieng, Vientiane Province, has taken the value of the product to a much higher level. Machinery cuts the mulberry paper into fine strips and twists it so that the result resembles thin string (left). This is then woven together with cotton for the warp (right), into attractive place mats (below) for a most unusual souvenir.

Other Interesting Occupations

95

Kapok. This tree, *Ceiba pentandra*, is an African native that has been planted in gardens around Southeast Asia for a long time. It is identifiable even in the non-fruiting season by its typically green trunk and branches, but its desirability lies in its fruit, which is a large pod (near right); Vientiane. As the dry season progresses, the green pods turn brown when ripened (far right); they are then harvested, and cottony contents removed (below); Don Det, Khong District, Champasak Province. The resulting material is used for stuffing pillows and mattresses (below right); Pak Lai District, Sayabouli Province. If your mattress here is not springy, then almost certainly it is stuffed with kapok.

Brooms. In late January and early February, a tall, wild roadside grass named *Thysanolaena latifolia* matures (above left); identified by JF Maxwell. This grass is prized for its elongate seedheads, which are turned into household brooms. Great bundles of the grass are harvested and carried back to the villages (above center), where available surfaces including road shoulders and bridge abutments are used for drying. At the same time, the seeds must be removed, which is a family affair; seeds are sometimes extracted by rolling the seed head (above right). All Vang Vieng District, Vientiane Province. Much more often, flailing the grass bundles to swat the seeds out is seen (center right); Khamkeut District, Bolikhamsai Province. While all of the collecting, flailing and drying is a cottage industry, the product of all this labor may then be taken to a cooperative (below right) for further processing; Kasi District. The end result is the household brooms for sale in urban centers, on display together with street brooms and litter baskets (below); Vientiane.

Other Interesting Occupations

Horticulture. Plants that are cultivated for household gardens here are commercially pantropical, with most varieties originally imported from elsewhere. Some native exceptions to this may be lotus, water lilies, and orchids. The major urban centers have nurseries that are fun to visit, the most convenient being the retail stalls forming a whole lane of their own just outside the outer wall of the That Luang Temple compound in Vientiane (above left). Their stock includes the desert rose, *Adenium obesum* (above right), native of the Arabian peninsula. Marigolds, *Tagetes patula*, are widely grown in private gardens (below left in Champasak) and as a crop due to their religious significance; they are sold as temple offerings (below right) on appropriate occasions; Vientiane.

Lao Close Encounters

Pendulous *Brugmansia* flowers (above left) are part of the landscaping at Khouangsi Waterfall outside Luang Prabang. *Poinsettia* and *Bougainvillea* (above right) hide an entire house behind them in Vang Vieng District, Vientiane Province; note child's face in lower right corner for scale. Cassava is both an edible root and a garden plant, able to grow quickly to create privacy (below left); Vientiane. If space and resources are available, a water lily fishpond may be created (below right); Luang Prabang.

Other Interesting Occupations

Epiphytic orchids of many species are gathered in the forests (though there may also be commercial varieties), and transplanted by wiring onto surfaces around houses (below); Hongsa/Ngeun District, Sayabouli Province. Oxcarts (*kian*) are very rarely seen in their original capacity any longer, but instead they are used as attractive planters (right); Outhoumphon District, Savannakhet Province. In May, flame trees (*Delonix regia*) light up the roadsides here and there (below right); Thapangthong District, Savannakhet Province.

Lao Close Encounters

Construction. With a rapidly expanding population, the building industry is thriving. Techniques and materials are appropriate to the size of the job. In rural areas the grass-roofed bamboo house still serves villagers well. Gathering and carrying the thatching grass can be an exhausting job (above); Kham District, Sieng Khouang Province. The grass is woven into panels, then passed up to make the necessary dry season (March) repairs to the roof (right); skilled hands receive the panel and secure it from the inside (below); Sienghon District, Sayabouli Province. Of course the time comes when repairs are not enough and the whole roof is replaced (below right); Bachiangcharoensouk District, Champasak Province.

Other Interesting Occupations

More upscale are wooden structures. With the forest still available, this involves sawing logs into boards. It is simply a matter of drawing a line on a log and following it with a 2-man saw (above left); near Luang Nam Tha. Want the job to get done twice as fast? Sawyers may start at opposite ends of the log and follow the same line to the center (above right); Vientiane Capital.

Still more upscale are concrete buildings in towns and cities. When they need repair, the scaffolding is likely to be bamboo (below left); Luang Prabang. For new concrete buildings, one of the early steps is to erect scaffolding that resembles a dense forest of saplings (below right); Vientiane.

Lao Close Encounters

Bamboo, Rattan, Wickerwork. In its simplest form, bamboo may be split along its length and woven into sections (above) to make fences or even house walls; Vientiane. Rattan may be slit into fine strips and woven into drinking glass coasters and other useful household items. New tray bottoms are being cut (right), while the president of the Ban Nongheo handicraft group (left) proudly displays some of the larger finished trays; Hatsaifong District, Vientiane Capital. A wide variety of nicely finished wickerwork is available, shown (below) at a festival exhibition in Vientiane.

Other Interesting Occupations

Woodworking. Decorative items are created by skilled artisans. The elephants (below) are intended for the upper corners of door jambs; Ban Phanom, Luang Prabang.

Enormous burls (right) and inverted tree stumps (below right) are turned into objects of art in Vientiane; these will not fit into your suitcase, but shipping is available.

Lao Close Encounters

The availability of wood means that furniture craftsmen can make their products beautiful but incredibly heavy (right); Vang Vieng District, Vientiane Province. Riverine villages such as this one on the bank of the Nam Khan River may have a resident boat builder (below), clearly a utilitarian craft; Ban Sieng Lom outside Luang Prabang. Delving deeply into his subject, this artisan chisels away at the inside of a huge tree trunk (below right) in order to create a new temple drum; Thoulakhom District, Vientiane Province.

Other Interesting Occupations

Distilling. This too is widely undertaken as a cottage industry. The product is rice whiskey, and the process is most easily observed in villages along the Mekong River just above Luang Prabang (above right), where children are in charge of the process. It is also a family affair just outside Luang Nam Tha (below right). At the other end of the scale, the biggest distiller of all is this factory (above left) in Hatsaifong District, Vientiane Capital, and its familiar product containers (below left).

106   Lao Close Encounters

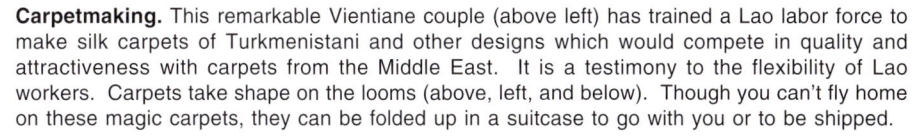

Carpetmaking. This remarkable Vientiane couple (above left) has trained a Lao labor force to make silk carpets of Turkmenistani and other designs which would compete in quality and attractiveness with carpets from the Middle East. It is a testimony to the flexibility of Lao workers. Carpets take shape on the looms (above, left, and below). Though you can't fly home on these magic carpets, they can be folded up in a suitcase to go with you or to be shipped.

Other Interesting Occupations 107

Weaving. This tradition is absolutely alive and well in Laos. It requires the preliminary steps of raising silkworms, boiling their pupal cocoons to loosen the silk strands (above left) so that they may be spun into thread, and dyeing the product, desirably with natural dyes from berries, leaves, bark, and minerals, to make it ready for the loom; Vientiane. The looming typically takes place on the ground under the weaver's stilted house. There is little danger of the weaving tradition being lost, as it is undertaken by senior citizens, young women, and even girls after school (below left, above, and below); Ban Phanom outside Luang Prabang.

Lao Close Encounters

Although weaving is done throughout the country, it is much more common in the northern provinces. Practitioners show their style in Ngeun District, Sayabouli Province (above left); Viangthong District, Houa Phan Province (right); Ban Phanom, Luang Prabang (center left); and the Lanten tribe shows its method outside the town of Luang Nam Tha (below left). All that is left to do is to bargain for price on all of the beautiful pieces (below right); Ban Phanom, Luang Prabang.

Other Interesting Occupations 109

Functional produce of the loom: for Boloven Plateau maiden (far left) in Paksong District, Champasak Province, Vientiane shopkeeper (near left) or Vientiane schoolgirls (below), the dress standard is still the *sinh*, resulting in all of them looking quite elegant.

Brickmaking. Under the topsoil of the rolling plains of Pek District, Sieng Khouang Province, the clay is just the right consistency for making bricks (above left). The clay is removed, piled, and then passed through a machine that extrudes it like spaghetti in a continuous line the right width and height for bricks; it is then cut with fine wire into the correct length for bricks, several at a time, and loaded into a handcart (above right). The brick-shaped clay is then stacked in rows for sun drying (left). A pyre-like structure is then created with old brick below and new sun-dried clay above, with many interstices that allow for the free flow of hot air from the fire underneath (below left). The "cooked" stack is now worthy of being called bricks, and is ready to be hauled off to construction sites (below).

Other Interesting Occupations

Factory Hands. With the exception of major sawmills and other industries that exploit natural resources, factories tend to be an urban phenomenon. The population has expanded much faster than the people can be absorbed into productive work, and therefore with the exception of the rice planting season the Lao labor force is generally underemployed. Just as elsewhere, there is migration of labor from rural areas to urban centers, but existing factories are only able to absorb small numbers. Government policies increasingly encourage trade and foreign investment to set up joint ventures in order to create more jobs, all under the continually cited theme of poverty eradication/alleviation.

A Chinese joint venture manufactures cement in factories just south of Vang Vieng, Vientiane Province (top left), reducing dependence on Thailand. Tha Deua Road in Hatsaifong District, Vientiane Capital, is something of an industrial corridor, where tobacco (second left) and joint venture beer (third left) enterprises are centered. While there is no doubt that these industries make large contributions to the state budget as well as creating employment opportunities, and are therefore encouraged, there is irony in that they come at the expense of local consumers who may develop health problems or increase accidents.

Any more room in there? A factory truck/bus (bottom left) picks up its labor force along 103 Hospital Road, Vientiane, in the morning. Clothing factory hands, some still with pink work aprons, patronize a food vendor (bottom right) at lunchtime along Luang Prabang Road, Vientiane. The shirt label (below) is new; no doubt the world will be seeing more of it in the future.

112 Lao Close Encounters

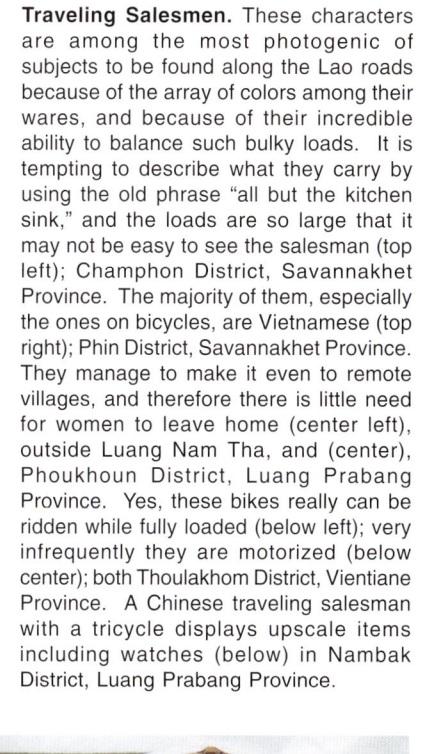

Traveling Salesmen. These characters are among the most photogenic of subjects to be found along the Lao roads because of the array of colors among their wares, and because of their incredible ability to balance such bulky loads. It is tempting to describe what they carry by using the old phrase "all but the kitchen sink," and the loads are so large that it may not be easy to see the salesman (top left); Champhon District, Savannakhet Province. The majority of them, especially the ones on bicycles, are Vietnamese (top right); Phin District, Savannakhet Province. They manage to make it even to remote villages, and therefore there is little need for women to leave home (center left), outside Luang Nam Tha, and (center), Phoukhoun District, Luang Prabang Province. Yes, these bikes really can be ridden while fully loaded (below left); very infrequently they are motorized (below center); both Thoulakhom District, Vientiane Province. A Chinese traveling salesman with a tricycle displays upscale items including watches (below) in Nambak District, Luang Prabang Province.

Other Interesting Occupations

113

Jewelers, Silversmiths. Silver and gold jewelry is readily available in urban marketplaces, which may be made locally or imported. However, visiting the workshops may not be so easy. The jewelry being made here (above left, above right, and left) is at a development enterprise in Vientiane. Silver bowls (right) are crafted by an artisan in Luang Prabang. A young goldsmith (below) works in the main market in Ponsawan, the administrative center of Sieng Khouang Province.

Artists. Painting pictures as art does not seem to be particularly popular as yet. There are some painters, but their work is not easy to locate. One prolific artist has recently had his work on exhibit for sale inside the rear wall of the That Luang compound, Vientiane (left and above), though such an arrangement is not likely to be permanent. There is also a gallery with the work of various artists on display in Vientiane (below left). Most artistic people express their creativity in other ways, especially in weaving and woodworking. A machinery welder with some extra time on his hands tries out a little of his own form of expression (below); Vientiane.

Other Interesting Occupations

TRAVEL

Travel by Air. A number of exotic destinations can be reached from Vientiane's Wattay International Airport (above left). In addition to those listed on the board (center left), Siem Reap and Chiang Mai (both with one stop) are also served. The Lao fleet description now shows an Airbus 320, which however did not appear on a recent schedule. The morning Thai flight from Bangkok (above right) is popular with the Western community. A major upgrade of the runway to accommodate Boeing 747s was made with Thai government financing and grants just before the November 2004 ASEAN Summit, perhaps in anticipation of a quantum leap in tourist arrivals.

For domestic flights, ten of the seventeen provincial/administrative capitals have scheduled passenger service; the other seven are either too close to Vientiane city to warrant having their own, or they lack the population base to require one. A dual ticket price structure is used.

For most routes the best you can hope for is a French ATR 72 (right center and bottom right). Other aircraft include several tiny Chinese Y 12 aircraft mainly serving the mountainous northern provinces, but there may still be an elderly Chinese Y 7 (bottom left) rolled out if necessary. In a recent upgrade of their public image, the name of the fleet has changed from the stolid "Lao Aviation" to the friendlier "Lao Airlines," with a new logo and paint job to complete the makeover, as seen (bottom right) at the Oudomsai airport.

116 Lao Close Encounters

Travel by Water. Before the advent of roads and tracks, following the water courses by boat was clearly the line of least resistance as compared to trekking through the forest in order to get into the country's interior. The rivers were facilitators rather than obstacles. The French explorers' accounts of Indochina in the latter half of the 1800s, now readily available in translation from several Asian-based publishers, are full of stories about river travel. Even now during the rainy season the watercourses may be the only way to get into various places. Pirogues (above), here seen on the Nam Khan River near Luang Prabang, may be polled or paddled across the river, between villages, or out to where the fishing is best. These pirogues may also be fitted with a motor for longer distance travel, such as (below) on the Nam Tha River at Luang Nam Tha.

Boats from the sky: on the Nam Thoen River, Khamkeut District, Bolikhamsai Province, sleek, maneuverable aluminum boats are used (above left and left) that are fabricated from jettisonable jet fuel tanks (below left) dropped here by the Americans during the Vietnam War. Why only here? The fuel tanks are apparently still being found after 30+ years; the word "DRAIN" can still be read next to the small hole in this one.

Travel

117

Ferries to take you across the rivers come in many sizes from the simple pirogue to ones that carry fully loaded oil tankers and logging trucks. The one (above) is two pirogues, one with a motor, joined by a platform on which the passengers stand; Longsan District, Vientiane Province. Did a pink umbrella salesman just come through?

Whenever new bridges are completed (below), ferries go out of business; Se Kaman River, Saisettha District, Attapeu Province. Larger ferries are alive and well on the Mekong River, where there are still only two bridges involving Laos, though a third is being built now.

Want to have a ride on a funky ferry? There is one on the Nam Ngoum River (above) about 60 kilometers north of Vientiane, on the way to the Nam Ngoum Dam. It runs all year round, but the color of the River is not the same in late June (below) as it is in April; Thoulakhom District, Vientiane Province.

Strictly for pleasure: there is an evening beer cruise on the Mekong River that departs from the Vientiane waterfront (below). See also Bokeo Province for other river travel.

Lao Close Encounters

Mekong River. While the specifics of boat travel will be mentioned under the various provinces, some generalizations about the river may be appropriate here. It is said to be the 12th largest river in the world, runs some 1800 kilometers along or through Laos, and has 17 Lao tributaries. It is tremendously important to the people who live anywhere near it, in terms of fishing, irrigation, and of course transportation. Biologists have determined the broad extent of the diversity of species living in it. It is also said that only 20% of the river's volume comes from China (Vientiane Times, 16 June 2004). Yet China has manipulated the river in very controversial ways both within and beyond its own borders by building dams (completed and planned) and by funding the blasting of "shoals, rapids and reefs" to facilitate the travel of heavier boats from the China border at least downstream as far as Chiang Khong, Thailand, opposite Ban Houai Sai, Bokeo. The arguments against such activities are that the downstream volume may be affected, that fishing stocks may be harmed by environmental changes and pollution, that banks may be more subject to erosion, and that international boundaries may be influenced. But the blasting is already nearly completed, and the dam building will continue. The last several years have seen extremes of exceptional flooding and drought on the river. Whether anything is to blame other than rainfall differences is debatable. The second-highest recorded flood stage was on 19 August 2002 (second only to 1966); while a 40+ year low level record was set in March 2003 (second only to 1960), repeated in 2004. During the highest water and rains, non-river transport was disrupted and crops and houses flooded; during the lowest, navigation was halted between Vientiane and southern Sayabouli Province, and Vientiane's taps and water plants could not meet the demand. A full-length Mekong River descent (by kayak) was completed for the first time by an Australian consultant residing in Vientiane (Vientiane Times, 12 October 2004).

The seasons of the river are nowhere more easily observed than at Vientiane. It is situated on a bend in the river including a wide sandbar that, in drought and standing at its edge, the Thai bank seems nearby (above left) as compared to the Lao shoreline (above right). In flood the river is an awesome spectacle (below left). After an earlier flood had inundated much of Vientiane, an earthen dike was built to protect the city; while the 2002 flood took bites out of the dike (right), it held the water back (below center) and the corniche remained dry (both B. Schofield photos). Houses built between the river and the dike on the upstream end of town suffered flood damage.

Travel 119

What is a "temporary" island? It is one that, during the dry season, has a "channel" that turns into rich bottomland for vegetable crops (above left), its fertility having been replenished by the river. Even in the dry season, although the "island" is connected throughout its length, it is still easier to take the bridge back to the mainland (above). During July the level of the Mekong River rises to the extent that the temporary channel is flowing insistently, making Don Chan Island worthy of its name, and the villagers must harvest their last produce from the low ground (left). In August at the peak of the rainy season the villagers living on the island never quite know how much of their fields will remain above water, and in 2002, there was almost nothing left dry (below left). In 2004 the hydrological situation changed when the entire upstream end of the island and the channel were filled in and a 14-story hotel, Vientiane's tallest building, was constructed (below).

A river runs through it: this villager's house, that is (above left), on Don Chan Island. Most of the village houses have two stories, but even so this flood was so intense that 60 of the 84 houses were temporarily evacuated (Vientiane Times, 23 August 2002). A village boy takes the situation in stride (above center). No matter what the season, the river takes its toll of the island (above right and right). Looking upstream from the bridge during the flood, it's water everywhere (below). Small wonder that most people scratched their heads when, in March 2004, the upper end of the channel was filled in to begin the new hotel (previous page); Vientiane.

Travel

121

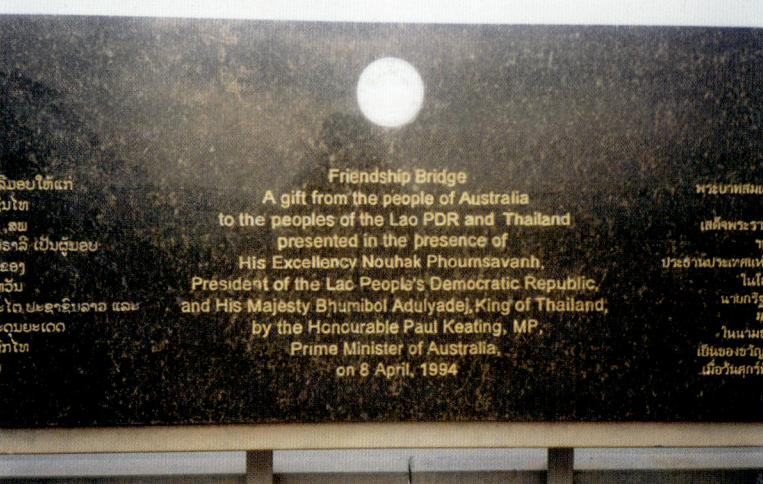

Travel by Rail. We all know that there isn't any yet, at least not since the 1947 demise of the French two-island railway that avoided the Mekong River Falls near Cambodia. But there was supposed to be rail travel, and the government even has a Lao Railway Authority. The Friendship Bridge over the Mekong between Hatsaifong District, Vientiane Capital, and Nong Khai, Thailand (top left), a gift from Australia, was opened on 8 April 1994 (top right). There were 10th anniversary celebrations commemorating the opening, with flags flying in the middle signifying the friendship of the three nations (center left). But the commemoration reiterated the original intentions of the bridge, which included "a proposed rail link between Vientiane and Bangkok and, eventually, a link to southern China and Vietnam" (Vientiane Times, 8 April 2004), and it was also explained that the passage of a train is why the bridge was designed to be so flat. With hope, at the time of bridge construction the Thai government extended its northeastern rail line from the Nong Khai station up onto the bridge (above), right up to its very center at the international line of demarcation, where it stops dead in its tracks (left).

Lao Close Encounters

Travel by Road. After joining the Association of Southeast Asian Nations (ASEAN) and developing "Visit Laos Year 1999-2000," the country swallowed its earlier introspection in favor of welcoming tourists (and even ex-citizens) and their hard currencies. Since that time, there is almost nowhere that officialdom has stood in the way of travel, even in the remotest areas. The only exception that readily comes to mind was the extreme southeast corner of the Boloven Plateau. The restrictions are physical rather than official, making Laos a country filled with sheer adventure for those with the time, health and resources to tackle it. The story told by the photos in this section, perhaps more than any other, is a portrait in time which is changing with breathtaking speed. The government's road development program is extremely ambitious, funded by international organizations such as the Asian Development Bank, or by grants in aid from various distant donor nations, or sometimes by agreements with three neighbors. Laos envisions itself as a trade gateway nation, with transit routes going in all directions (Vientiane Times, 22 March 2002), and it has come a very long way in a few short years. Many roads previously requiring endless slogs through the mud are now all-weather roads with proper bridges, facilitating trade and communication as never before, and, yes, in a way diminishing the adventurous aspect.

In all fairness to the government, when such a large percentage of the country is mountainous it stands to reason that road building is problematic and costly. Road maintenance is required far more frequently, and quick response to road problems is not the expected norm. In addition to the standard motoring problems encountered everywhere, such as drivers falling asleep, drunk drivers and vehicles that are not roadworthy, there are a whole host of special problems here. Many of them relate to the season: in the rainy season the roads are very slippery, or have deep mud and impassable river fords. In the dry season there is deep dust and sand. There is the problem of the incongruous range of vehicles that share the roads, everything from fully loaded logging trucks and long distance buses to tractor carts and bicycles.

There is the problem of large numbers of young and inexperienced drivers who are able to afford Chinese motorbikes that cost little more than $400, and an expansion of the traffic volume just as the population expands. There is the problem of visibility not only as a result of rain or dust but around mountainous or vegetated curves, and with completely unlighted vehicles (tractor carts without as much as a reflector) in the middle of high speed lanes at night. There is the problem of road surface conditions, including landslides, washouts and damaged bridges, commonly without any advance visual cues or warning signs. There are obstacles on the road surface, including domestic animals, fallen trees, fallen rock, construction activities, and drying commodities. Then there are peculiar interpretations of the protocol of the road, including behavior at roundabouts and the "invisible third lane." There is little horn honking here, as it is considered impolite. The moral of the story is, just go slow. Mercifully, you will immediately note that the Lao do just that, as compared with their more intense neighbors. Filling stations are rare in remote areas, and a good principle would be to keep the tank topped up whenever the opportunity presents itself. The Lao are wonderfully helpful people, so if you are going to break down, it pays to do it near human habitation, and don't take extra risk after the time that the farmers have returned home. All available road maps have some good and some unreliable features. There are a number of them on the market (at least five), but not one gives a consistently accurate picture of what can be expected. They may show passable river crossings where there is no way to get across, no matter what the season, or fail to show the presence of perfectly good roads that were in existence years before their date of publication. One partial solution: buy one of each and consult all of them. This would also provide the advantage of seeing where the National Protected Areas (NPA) are on one, or mountainous area shading on another, or the district centers and boundaries on another, or have the convenience of a booklet format with another, etc. An entire book could, and should, be written about motoring in Laos.

Government statistics show that as of last year Laos had 4497 km of asphalted roads, 10,097 km of graveled roads, and 16,616 km of dirt roads (Vientiane Times, 6 December 2004). The country's best roads are Route 13 South from Vientiane to the Cambodian border, here shown at a rare leafy stretch in Savannakhet Province that has attracted roadside stands (left), and Route 9 across Savannakhet Province, built to international standard as the Lao portion of the Trans-Asia Highway, here shown in Outhoumphon District (above).

If you call the curve in the photo (above right) a hairpin turn, what do you call the curve in the other photo (right)? Both are on Route 7, in Phoukout District, Sieng Khouang Province, and Phoukhoun District, Luang Prabang Province, respectively.

Travel

Seasonality problems: a period of heavy rain may produce this result on Setthathilat Road in Vientiane in June (above left), but all it takes is a light rain in the mountains to make the asphalt road surfaces very slippery. You never know just how deep the mud is until you plunge in (above); June in Tonpheung District, Bokeo Province. There comes a time in October when the rivers may again be low enough to ford; if you're the bus, you have lots of built-in help when you get stuck (left); Khamkeut District, Bolikhamsai Province.

The opposite problem: in the dry season, the dust raised by passing (or preceding) vehicles is amazing, reducing the visibility to almost nothing (center right) and forcing motorists to "eat" each other's dirt; March in Mounlapamok District, Champasak Province. In Vientiane and vicinity, there are some sprinkler trucks to help keep the dust settled, such as on the road to Tat Moon Falls (right), which boys can take advantage of as a moving shower on a hot day (photo B. Schofield).

Lao Close Encounters

Diversity of vehicles sharing the roads: long-distance buses await their departure time at the northern bus depot in Vientiane, headed for Sam Neua, Phongsali, and Sayabouli, respectively (top left). Inter-district truck/buses generally look something like this (top right); Sanasomboun District, Champasak Province. For villages off the paved roads, there's nothing like a high-clearance Russian-type truck/bus (center left) for getting through the mud and the rivers; Khoun/Thathom Road (Route 1), Khoun District, Sieng Khouang Province. These Chinese hybrid trucks with tractor engines (center) are seen in the northwestern provinces; Sieng Ngeun District, Luang Prabang Province. In urban areas, especially Vientiane, 3-wheeled *tuk-tuk* are convenient (center right); note that there are two types, the smaller ones having larger wheels. You can never be sure who the previous customer was (right). For transportation between villages, it's the tractor cart (below left); these are the ones that may be found even on main highways at night with not as much as a reflector on the back; Pathoumphon District, Champasak Province. What a rare treat to see an oxcart (*kian*) still in use (below center); Thoulakhom District, Vientiane Province.

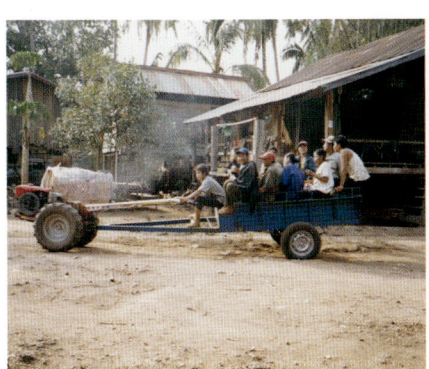

Travel

Paradise on earth: the Nam Et National Protected Area (NPA) sits atop the Annamite Mountains, but vegetation around curves reduces visibility (left), requiring very slow driving; Viangthong District, Houa Phan Province. More hazards: landslides come down from above (above center); Kham District, Sieng Khouang Province. Landslide below "eats" a lane out of Route 13 North (above right), and a land slump in progress takes the southbound lane (center) at a curve in the road without warning signs; both Sieng Ngeun District, Luang Prabang Province. Eventually the bulldozer arrives and cuts the road farther back into the mountainside. A washout takes more than half the road surface (center right) in Sanakham District, Vientiane Province; this time some kind souls have alerted motorists to the hazard with bamboo, but this is the exception rather than the rule.

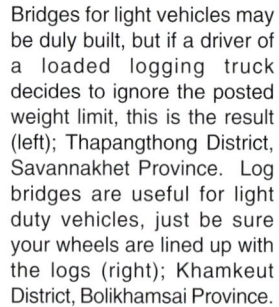

Bridges for light vehicles may be duly built, but if a driver of a loaded logging truck decides to ignore the posted weight limit, this is the result (left); Thapangthong District, Savannakhet Province. Log bridges are useful for light duty vehicles, just be sure your wheels are lined up with the logs (right); Khamkeut District, Bolikhamsai Province.

Lao Close Encounters

The roads belong to the cattle, and they are reluctant to move (top left) to allow for the passage of anything else; Khoun District, Sieng Khouang Province. They sometimes seem to arrange themselves as an obstacle course, but the bus driver is equal to the task without hesitation (top right); Hin Boun District, Khammouan Province. It is always a thrill to see a sight like this on the road ahead (center left); Long District, Luang Nam Tha Province. Dead trees and old logs may fall onto the road surface from above, with nobody concerned enough to clear them away as long as a passable lane remains open (center right); Sam Neua District, Houa Phan Province. What happens when a tree falls across the road while you are in the hinterlands and have to get back out? Try to hire somebody to chop it out of the way (right), even if it is at night and raining; Phouvong District, Attapeu Province. Rock fall from above can occur at any time; a few bluffs overhang the road (left); Khamkeut District, Bolikhamsai Province.

Travel

Construction delays can occur as a result of road building activity (right), but bulldozer operators are generally considerate about not interrupting traffic for too long; Phoukout District, Sieng Khouang Province. Road surfaces are tempting places to dry grain (center right); Route 13 South, Khong District, Champasak Province.

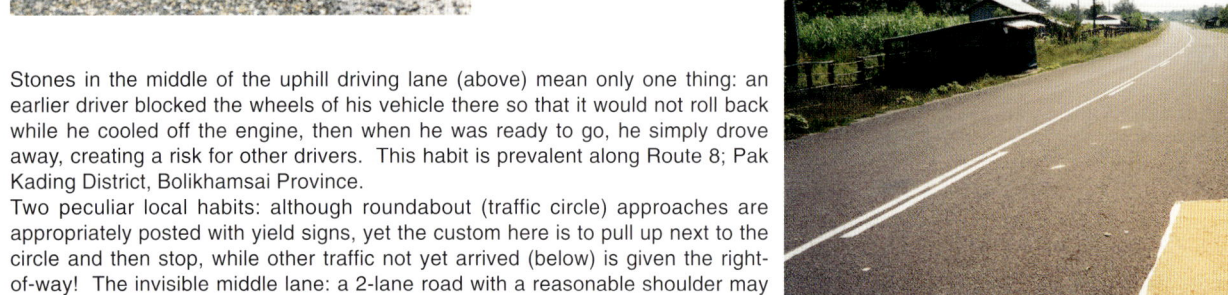

Stones in the middle of the uphill driving lane (above) mean only one thing: an earlier driver blocked the wheels of his vehicle there so that it would not roll back while he cooled off the engine, then when he was ready to go, he simply drove away, creating a risk for other drivers. This habit is prevalent along Route 8; Pak Kading District, Bolikhamsai Province.

Two peculiar local habits: although roundabout (traffic circle) approaches are appropriately posted with yield signs, yet the custom here is to pull up next to the circle and then stop, while other traffic not yet arrived (below) is given the right-of-way! The invisible middle lane: a 2-lane road with a reasonable shoulder may turn into a 3-lane road at any time that someone decides to pass despite the fact that there is oncoming traffic (below right). Everybody seems to understand this and just takes it in stride by getting over. Vientiane.

Lao Close Encounters

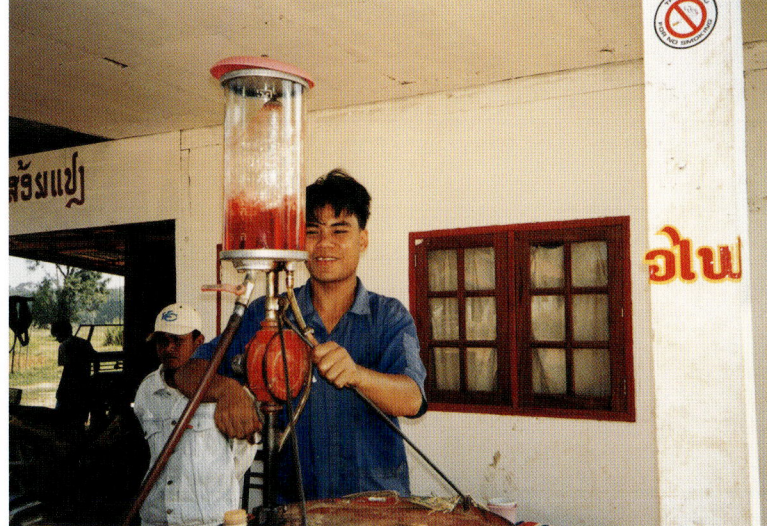

Filling stations: while there are full-service modern stations in urban areas (like Vientiane, above left), in rural areas you are more likely to see fuel hand-cranked out of a barrel and up into a 5-liter cylinder for measuring, then run to your tank through a hose (above right); Sonbouli District, Savannakhet Province. Motorbikes and small machines are seen all over, and their fuel may be sold in pop bottles (center left), which in time of dire need will serve for larger vehicles too; Pak Kading District, Bolikhamsai Province. For simple jobs like changing tires, it can be done by small town mechanics even barefooted (below left); Soukhouma District, Champasak Province. For difficult work, it might take an international mechanic (below center); Vientiane. Three who did not succeed in avoiding all the risks (right): this off-duty bus went over a cliff and rolled down perhaps a hundred meters, and was later brought back up; Phoukhoun District, Luang Prabang Province. The log hauling truck lost its brakes in the mountains and the driver lived by jackknifing the rig inward toward the hillside; Sieng Ngeun District, Luang Prabang Province. The heavy equipment truck failed to make a curve; Vang Vieng District, Vientiane Province. Go slow!

Travel   129

NATURE

Flora. This section is to provide a small sample of the attractive plant species that may be encountered along Lao roadsides and trails. Some seasons are better than others for flowering native plants, especially February to May, but some species bloom in October and November. Thanks to Professor J.F. Maxwell of Chiang Mai University, Thailand, for identifying the species from photos.

Cut but unprocessed logs provide the substrate for a colorful variety of fungal growth; left column top to bottom: *Hexagonia tenuis* in Champasak District, *Stereum ostrea* in Nasaithong District of Vientiane Capital, and *Coprinus disseminatus* in Viangthong District of Houa Phan Province. The white heads of *Eriocaulon* (probably *E. sexangulare*) cover fallow rice fields in Soukhouma District, Champasak Province in October, creating an overall effect that is as close to looking snowy as it gets (above). A wetland of *Nelumbo nucifera*, the sacred lotus, thrives in Houai Sai District, Bokeo Province in June (below).

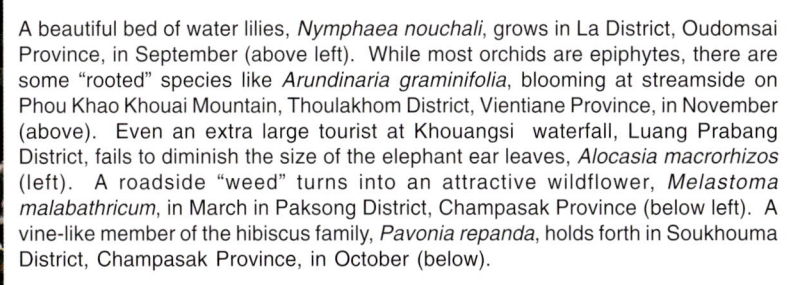

A beautiful bed of water lilies, *Nymphaea nouchali*, grows in La District, Oudomsai Province, in September (above left). While most orchids are epiphytes, there are some "rooted" species like *Arundinaria graminifolia*, blooming at streamside on Phou Khao Khouai Mountain, Thoulakhom District, Vientiane Province, in November (above). Even an extra large tourist at Khouangsi waterfall, Luang Prabang District, fails to diminish the size of the elephant ear leaves, *Alocasia macrorhizos* (left). A roadside "weed" turns into an attractive wildflower, *Melastoma malabathricum*, in March in Paksong District, Champasak Province (below left). A vine-like member of the hibiscus family, *Pavonia repanda*, holds forth in Soukhouma District, Champasak Province, in October (below).

Nature

The ginger family can be spectacular. One member, *Alpinia malaccensis* (above), grows 2 meters tall in Phoun District, Saisomboun Special Zone, in April. A short relative, *Curcuma zedoaria* (below), brightens rolling grasslands in Sam Neua District, Houa Phan Province, in May.

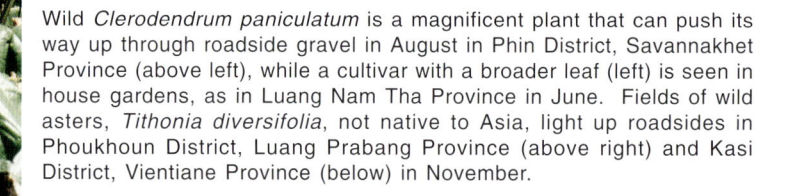

Wild *Clerodendrum paniculatum* is a magnificent plant that can push its way up through roadside gravel in August in Phin District, Savannakhet Province (above left), while a cultivar with a broader leaf (left) is seen in house gardens, as in Luang Nam Tha Province in June. Fields of wild asters, *Tithonia diversifolia*, not native to Asia, light up roadsides in Phoukhoun District, Luang Prabang Province (above right) and Kasi District, Vientiane Province (below) in November.

132

Lao Close Encounters

Senna alata (above), native to Asia but not originally Lao, graces the roadside in Vang Vieng District, Vientiane Province in November. Tree ferns (below) perhaps *Cyathea chinensis*, grow in the misty forest near the Vietnam border in Khamkeut District, Bolikhamsai Province.

Interesting bamboo, probably *Thyrostachys siamensis* (above), may be seen in some of the National Protected Areas such as Phou Phanang in Nasaithong District, Vientiane Capital. A *Corypha* palm, probably *C. umbraculifera* (left), towers over its surroundings in Nong Het District, Sieng Khouang Province. *Bauhinia variegata* trees come into full bloom in early March (below) on the hillsides, such as in Phoukhout District, Sieng Khouang Province. The flower of this genus may be the model for the logo of Hong Kong.

Nature

Another species of *Bauhinia* that grows almost vine-like (above left) occurs in the forest in Khamkeut District, Bolikhamsai Province, blooming in June, and could at first glance be mistaken for orchids. A *Lagerstroemia macrocarpa* tree (above center) is spectacular in April, growing in a pasture in the same district. Also in the same district, the tubular brilliant orange flowers of the *Radermachera ignea* tree (above right) are borne on the branches in March. *Cassia fistula*, the golden shower (left), is not native but it certainly beautifies Vientiane in April. Flame trees, *Delonix regia* (below), are always a treat to see at roadside; Vientiane Province.

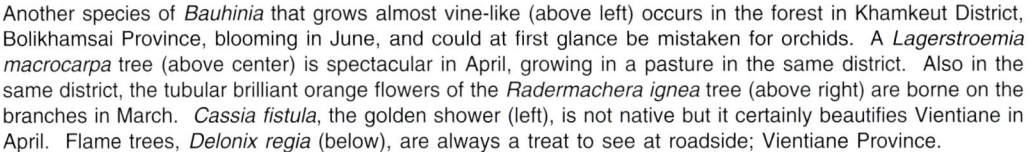

Cassia agnes (left), again not native here, devotes full energy to blooming in March in Pak Lai, Sayabouli Province. An old *Butea monosperma* tree (above), in full bloom in February, appears to be taking advantage of the presence of the adjacent outhouse in Tha Khaek District, Khammouan Province. The brilliant orange flowers of the small tree *Saraca indica* (below left) are highly photogenic in March in Pak Kading District, Bolikhamsai Province. This surviving forest giant, apparently *Bombax ceiba* (below center) flowers spectacularly in February in Luang Prabang District. Pine trees (below right) are the dominant vegetation in various highland areas including southeastern Khoun District, Sieng Khouang Province.

Nature

Fauna. Wildlife depends on forests, and as Laos harvests its timber resources the wild animal population takes a nosedive. The new roads being created for an expanding economy are good for trade and travel, but not good for the conservation of wildlife. Human population pressure creates encroachment into wildlife habitat. Hunters are clever and there is nothing "easy" left. As a result of all this, there is little expectation of seeing larger animals in the wild; instead they are seen in captivity (as pets or in the zoo) or for sale by the kilogram. The hunter-gatherer method of living off the land is still here. Seemingly everything is fair game to be hunted and to be eaten. Even villagers who have their own livestock may continue to prefer to eat wild game. Restaurants may have it available off-menu. The desire to eat game is often based on imagined medical, including aphrodisiacal, benefits. Just the same, as a result of its geographical remoteness, availability of the Annamites and other mountain ranges as refugia, 20th Century turmoil, and relatively low human density, the country's fauna taken as a whole is little known, and undescribed species (at least of invertebrates) abound. Conservation advocates assist the government's Ministry of Agriculture and Forestry to save what they can. There is a large-animal focus, and habitat conservation is paramount for the sake of fauna and flora alike. Some 20 National Biodiversity and Conservation Areas (NBCA), recently renamed National Protected Areas (NPA) have been established where development activities are discouraged. Wildlife trading laws have been passed, though enforcement is problematic. Advocates providing assistance include the Wildlife Conservation Society, Worldwide Fund for Nature, World Conservation Union, and several United Nations agencies. The trick is to find the balance between the needs of wildlife and those of man. Laos inventories 126 large mammals, 700 fowls, and 166 reptiles (Vientiane Times, 12 July 2002).

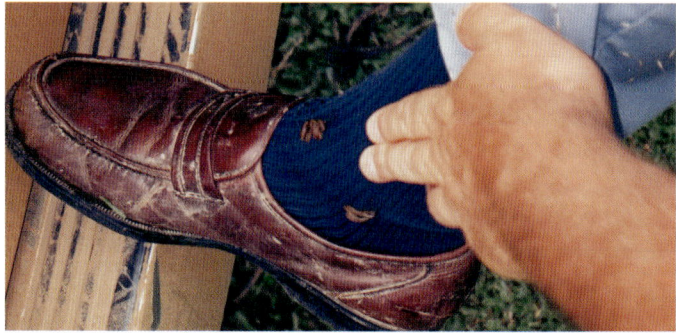

When is the "wildlife" happy to have you come by? When it's a parasite like the leech (top right) in Bolikhamsai Province. Groups of leeches in Houa Phan Province have the audacity to suck blood right through one's socks instead of waiting to locate bare skin (center right). Here's looking at you: a mountain crab ponders its predicament in Attapeu Province (above left), some 440 meters above sea level and 160 kilometers from the nearest seashore. The work of a spider is highlighted by morning dew (right) in Sieng Khouang Province. A termite colony attacking the bark of a living tree in Vientiane is observed when its protective covering of dried "mud" has just been tapped off (left).

Want to observe wild fauna? Think small! Insects are everywhere. Caddisflies (Trichoptera), in the midst of an amazing emergence from the nearby reservoir, find vehicle headlights irresistible (above left) in Vientiane Capital. A stink bug (Hemiptera) takes a rest (left center); bees and wasps (Hymenoptera) are common (bottom left). Beetles (Coleptera) are ubiquitous, but it may take some effort to find extra large ones like the dung beetle and rhinoceros beetle (above right), or the ones caught by a collector in Sieng Khouang Province (below center), members of the leucanid genus *Dorcus*. Blood-sucking flies (Diptera) of the genus *Tabanus* feed on the leg of a water buffalo (below right), Savannakhet Province.

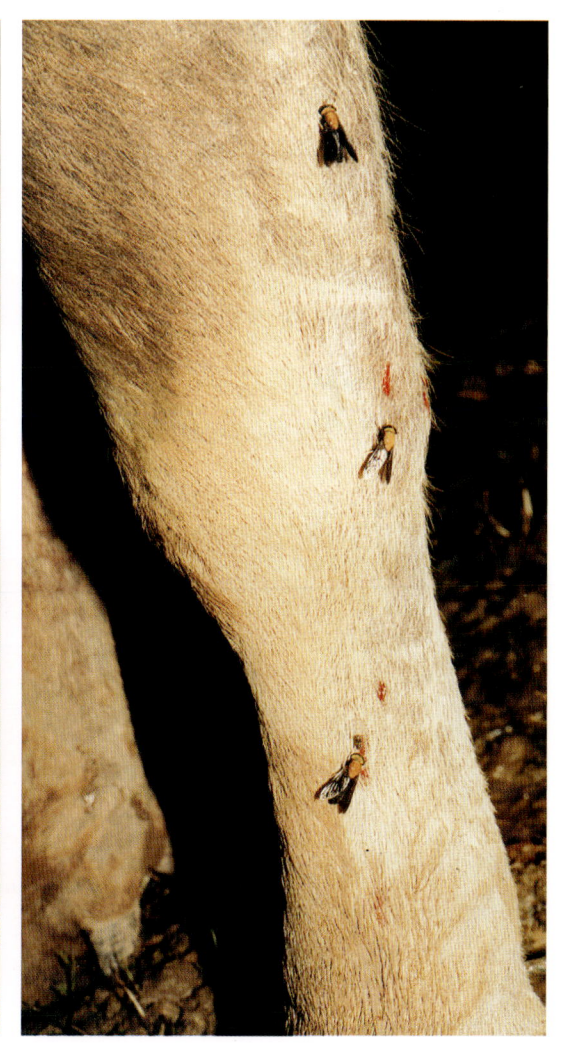

Nature

Butterflies, most people's favorite insect order (Lepidoptera), abound in Laos. One very interesting place is Tat Leuk Waterfall in Phou Khao Khouai NPA, Tha Phabat District, Bolikhamsai Province, where numerous species congregate (top left) to enjoy the same conditions. But roadside mud puddles are often attractive also, such as one (top right) in Nam Et NPA, Viangthong District, Houa Phan Province.
Portrait gallery: *Vindula erota* (above left), *Castalius rosimon* (above center), *Zeltus amasa* (above right), and a group mostly of brown-tipped *Eurema simulatrix* (below left), all in Khoun District, Sieng Khouang Province; a line (below right) containing *Appias lyncida*, first, fourth, and fifth from left, *Catopsilia pomona*, second left, and *Appias nero*, third left, in Dong Amphan NPA, Sansai District, Attapeu Province. All identifications courtesy of G.R. Ballmer.

Lao Close Encounters

Turtles are raised in a commercial pond (above) in Champhon District, Savannakhet Province. Monitor lizards (right) are kept alive for sale by roadside, Toumlan/Ta-Oy District, Salavan Province. Snakes may also be captured alive, as (below left) in Hin Hoep District, Vientiane Province; or they may be encountered in the wild, as this *Trimeresurus albolabris* (below right), the white-lipped pit viper, a dangerous species sheltering on a rock ledge along the Se Nam Noi River, Lamam District, Sekong Province.

What all the noise is about: males of *Gekko gecko* (above) "warm up" their voices first and then let fly with a series of "tok-kae," hence their common name. This specimen, in Pak Lai, Sayabouli Province, has had two reincarnations of its tail, after mishaps, and lived to tell the tale.

Nature

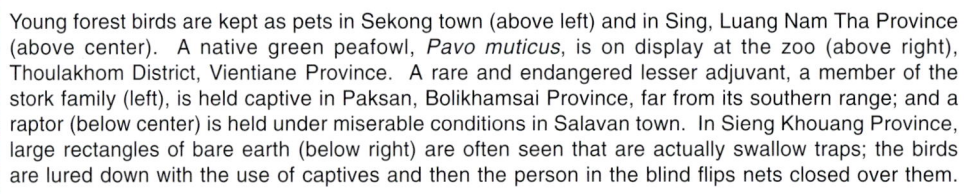

Young forest birds are kept as pets in Sekong town (above left) and in Sing, Luang Nam Tha Province (above center). A native green peafowl, *Pavo muticus*, is on display at the zoo (above right), Thoulakhom District, Vientiane Province. A rare and endangered lesser adjuvant, a member of the stork family (left), is held captive in Paksan, Bolikhamsai Province, far from its southern range; and a raptor (below center) is held under miserable conditions in Salavan town. In Sieng Khouang Province, large rectangles of bare earth (below right) are often seen that are actually swallow traps; the birds are lured down with the use of captives and then the person in the blind flips nets closed over them.

Lao Close Encounters

A hunter offers flying squirrels (above left), probably *Hylopetes alboniger*, in Nyommalat District, Khammouan Province. *Callosciurus* tree squirrels and a civet, apparently *Paguma larvata* (above center) are offered up to bus passengers, Sepon/Phin District, Savannakhet Province. *Rhizomys*, a bamboo rat (above right), is kept alive in an awkward position such that it is not able to chew through its tether in Sai District, Oudomsai Province. A roadside market in Pak Kading District, Bolikhamsai Province, offers live bats and dead rats (below right). Red-cheeked squirrels, *Dremomys rufigenis* (below left) are sold in Beng District, Oudomsai Province.

Nature

More individual sales along the road: a lesser Oriental chevrotain or mouse deer, *Tragulus javanicus* (left) in Beng District, Oudomsai Province; a serow, *Naemorhedus sumatraensis*, head (above left) and hide and desirable organs (above right) in Sepon District, Savannakhet Province; a red muntjac or barking deer, *Muntiacus muntjak* (below left) in Sai District, Oudomsai Province, and female (below center) and male (below right) of the same species still alive in the zoo, Thoulakhom District, Vientiane Province. A hog badger, *Arctonyx collaris* (right), this one making a surprise daytime appearance in a deep road cut, was seen in Khoun District, Sieng Khouang Province.

Lao Close Encounters

Irrawaddy dolphin country: the backs of several *Oracella brevirostris* (*pa kha*) may be seen in the center distance sticking out of the Mekong River (above left) near Veunkham, Khong District, Champasak Province, though there are no guarantees of seeing any, and the most accurate impression might come from the statue (above right) on the Cambodian side of the river. There are perhaps only 80 dolphins remaining today, where formerly there were thousands in the general area (Vientiane Times, 10 August 2004). A tiger, *Panthera tigris* (below left) is on display at Khouangsi Waterfall southwest of Luang Prabang; in the wild, they are still known to occur in the Annamite Mountains of western Houa Phan Province (Vientiane Times, 2 November 2004). Primates: villager with a shot slow loris, *Nycticebus coucang*, for sale (below center) in Sai District, Oudomsai Province; pygmy slow lorises, *Nycticebus pygmaeus* (bottom center) practice daytime energy conservation at the zoo, Thoulakhom District, Vientiane Province; a trusted family langur sits atop a wall with no tether (center right) in Vientiane; and a not-so-trusted rhesus macaque, *Macaca mulatta* (bottom right), is tethered in Pak Kading District, Bolikhamsai Province.

Nature

THE PROVINCES

Laos is proud of its record of attracting tourists since a change of policy in 1990 began to make visiting it a reasonable prospect. The peak year 2002 saw over 737,000 arrivals, generating US $113.8 million (Vientiane Times, 12 April 2004). Though there are, and will continue to be, bumps along the way such as SARS, bird flu, and economic turndowns, it would seem that the trend has nowhere to go but up, and that it will include visitation of a wider variety of destinations around the country. This section provides a taste of what can be expected on a province-by-province basis, calling attention to the unique features.

Attapeu Province. This province is the most distant from Vientiane and is among the most rural. It forms the southeastern corner of the country, having borders with Cambodia and Vietnam, and the area has recently been dubbed "the Diamond Triangle," in keeping with "the Golden Triangle" of the three countries touching at Bokeo Province. On the Ho Chi Minh Trail of the Vietnam War years, it comes first on the list of the UXO Lao nine most unexploded ordnance contaminated provinces (Vientiane Times, 4 May 2004), and this list is not simply in alphabetical order. Although the province has no international checkpoints for third-country nationals, it will soon have closer ties with Vietnam, which is funding a realigned Route 18 to its border in Kon Tum Province.

In the Dong Amphan National Protected Area, Sansai District, Route 18 used to be just a forest track (above left) but is being turned into a wide highway (above right). Simultaneously, much of the forest wildlife habitat (below left) is lost to logging for export eastward (below right) and to agriculture; Phouvong District.

Lao Close Encounters

Before and after: this is the road north of Attapeu town in 1998 (above) and the same road in the same general area in 2004 (above right). The tranquility of the Se Kaman River at Attapeu town (right) is broken only by the ripples of the ferries to and from Phouvong District. Bridge building is rampant: the new Se Kong River bridge at Attapeu town (below) makes the ferry landing to its left obsolete; and the new bridge over the Se Kaman River in Saisettha District (below right) also puts ferries out of business.

The Provinces

Not exactly beating swords into plowshares, but close: turning cluster bomb casings into onion beds (above left) in Phouvong District. Battleground of the superpowers: a Russian missile (above) on display in Sansai District. While tribes may dress in Lao or Western styles, their meeting hall architecture or totems (left) may provide clues to their ethnicity, as in Sanamsai District. The temple grounds in Attapeu town have a new set of interacting figures (below left); and the same grounds have a residence hall (below) with unusual architecture.

Lao Close Encounters

Bokeo Province. This province, more phonetically spelled Baw Kaew, has a bit of a naming problem. It was formerly called Houa Khong, head of the Mekong, but that was a misnomer so it was changed to Bokeo, gem mine. However, even though there is still some sapphire mining in Houai Sai District, the mines are not as productive as they once were, and so the new name is not particularly descriptive either. This is another province that borders two countries, Thailand and Burma, and is the Lao part of "the Golden Triangle." This name stems from the notorious opium trade in the area. Bokeo was declared opium free in 2004, though during the last decade it was "well known as a producer of opium" (Vientiane Times, 7 June 2004). The Thai side of the Mekong River is well-furnished with roads, so it is no surprise that trade across the border is brisk. Trade with China is increasing, and China has paid for the blasting of reefs and shoals in the Mekong River from its border down to the Thai border and Bokeo in order to improve navigation conditions for trade by its own larger ships. The project has been controversial from the beginning of the 2000 agreement due to concerns over changes in river ecology to the detriment of fish and the fishing industry, potential increases in erosion and pollution, and international boundary demarcation (Bangkok Post, 7 August 2002). Controversial or not, the blasting is almost completed down to Ban Houai Sai (Vientiane Times, 30 June 2004). Ban Houai Sai to Chiang Khong is an official international crossing.

Entering the province by land, the visitor is greeted by this sign (above left) on Route 3; the "93 km" was an afterthought and is the distance to Ban Houai Sai. This road, soon to become much better, has actually been good for a long time because there is a coal mine above the northern border close to this sign, and the road has had to be strong for the coal trucks heading for the Mekong River. A remaining forest giant along Route 3 (left) is a reminder of how it used to be. A road junction in Houai Sai District has a sign (below) that points the way to Meung, Bokeo's northernmost district, and this is the track to Meung (right); it would be much easier in the dry season. Along the way but still in Houai Sai District, limestone caves are encountered with huge flat-bottomed overhangs about 1.5 meters above the ground surface (above right).

The Provinces

The Ban Houai Sai waterfront is busy, with Lao cargo/house boats tied up in the foreground and a Thai vehicular ferry bringing a fuel tank truck across (above left). Do you see the international "do not enter" symbol in the photo (above)? Neither do many other first-time visitors to Ban Houai Sai, making this street a big source of revenue in violation fines. The sign, obliterated by tree leaves cleverly left uncut, obliges motorists to turn right here as the street suddenly becomes one-way without any other warning. The Mekong River is forever eroding its banks, and a shop in Ban Houai Sai has done what it can to slow down the process (left). A hilltop temple in Ban Houai Sai overlooks the town and the river (below left), Chiang Khong, Thailand, across. This is an unusual entrance arch to the temple grounds (below center) of a village along the Nam Tha River in western Pha-Oudom District. A huge ancient Buddha statue emerges from tall weeds (below) in the Mekong River's big bend country of southern Tonpheung District. As this area faces Chiang Saen, the center of an ancient civilization, it is no wonder that this side of the river shares in that heritage, and according to material in the National Museum, Vientiane, this area was once part of the ancient town of Souvannakhom Kham.

Lao Close Encounters

Three countries in one photo (left): the foreground is Chiang Saen District, Thailand; beyond a small stream is the last neck of Burma that touches the Mekong, with green trees; and beyond the Mekong are the Lao hills of Tonpheung District.

With Thai speedboats in the foreground and Tonpheung District in the background, a Lao cargo/house boat heads upstream (leftward) passing a Chinese cargo boat headed downstream, probably destined for Chiang Saen (center left).

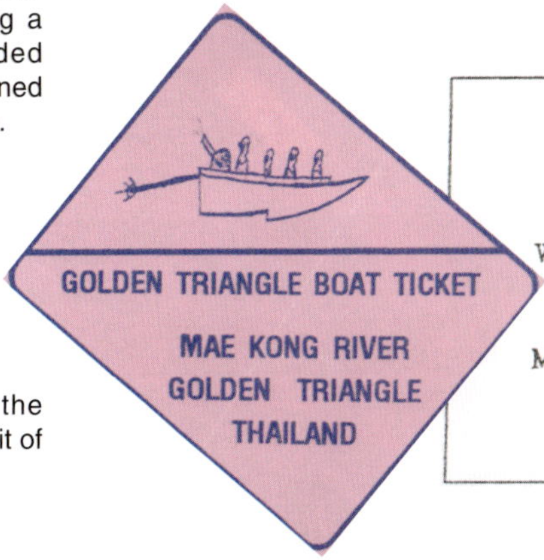

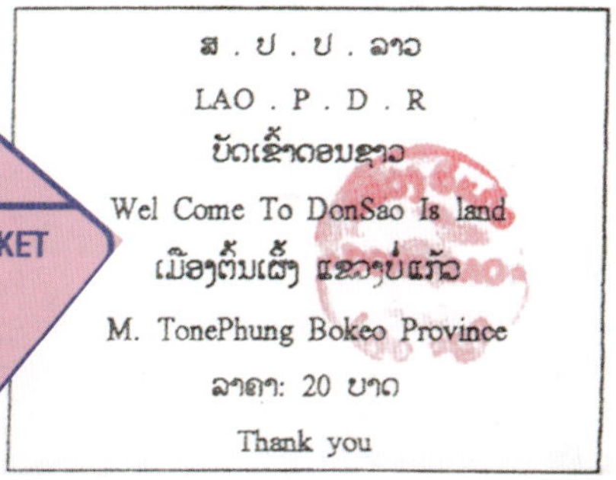

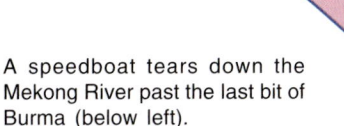

A speedboat tears down the Mekong River past the last bit of Burma (below left).

Would you like to set foot on Lao soil without a visa? Here's the place. It is Don Sao, a temporary island (connected to the Lao mainland except in the rainy season) and a part of Tonpheung District (top right). Find your way to Ban Sop Ruak (Golden Triangle Village), Chiang Saen District, Chiang Rai Province, Thailand. Then buy a boat ticket (center right, left side) and take a tour that includes Don Sao Island. When you arrive, just pay a small service fee (2004 price 20 baht) and get a chit (center right, right side) enabling you to walk around the island but not beyond. You can buy souvenirs and postage stamps, and then drop your postcards into the postal drop box (right) to prove that you've been there.

The Provinces

149

Bolikhamsai Province. This extends from the eastern border of Vientiane Capital at the Nam Ngoum River to Vietnam, and is important for trade and tourism as it is the shortest way east and is paved throughout, though some stretches are a hard climb for loaded trucks. The scenery is spectacular, though it would be more so if logging interests in the eastern part had not been so active. Tha Phabat, the westernmost district, has several claims to fame, namely its temples, the Naga fireballs, and Phou Khao Khouai (Buffalo Horn Mountain) National Protected Area. That Phabatphonsan stupa (above left), on Route 13 South, has a footprint of the Buddha, and the nearby Wat Naganimid is off to the south on the Mekong River. Both are revered and are pilgrimage sites for the faithful. The Naga fireballs (*Bang fai phayanak*) that emerge from the Mekong River in this district at the end of Buddhist Lent on the night of the October full moon are religiously considered to be the works of the Naga celebrating the occasion. You are not likely to hear any other version on the Lao side of the river, but the Tourism Authority of Thailand admits that there is a scientific explanation that requires a remarkable combination of conditions involving bacteria, water depth, organic deposits, bedding material, temperature and acidity to form methane gas that reacts with oxygen in the air and ignites. Phou Khao Khouai NPA visitor center is located at the beautiful Tat Leuk Waterfall (left, and below left), as seen here with rainy season flow in early October. Tat Sai Waterfall, in the same NPA, is seen here (above right) at the peak of the dry season in March. The Mekong River overflowed its banks in August 2002, with water crossing Route 13 South (below right) at a spot in Paksan District.

Lao Close Encounters

Route 8, an east-west road across southern Bolikhamsai Province (above left), with a lesser portion in northern Khammouan Province, provides a spectacular journey. It includes sights such as a natural arch (above center) and vertical limestone cliffs that appear to be knifepoint sharp at the top (above right). This Route 8 village (below left) in Pak Kading District may be vulnerable from the front, but it is exceptionally well defended from the rear. Khamkeut District has a "limestone forest" (below right) that appears to be impenetrable.

The Provinces

Route 1, the country's "interior" route, crosses several districts of Bolikhamsai in a northwesterly direction from the middle of Route 8. One of its first obstacles has been the Nam Ngouang River near its confluence with the Nam Thoen. If the water level is too low (top left), the vehicular ferry is beached; while if the level is too high, the ferry may be operable but the road condition will not allow you to go far, such as when road turns to river (left) in June in Viangthong District. Note that the Nam Ngouang ferry (above) is powered with poles, principally by young women. It is always a pleasure to see a raised onion bed that is *not* a cluster bomb casing (below left), Viangthong District. Several years ago, a major effort was made throughout the country to prepare village level land use planning maps such as this one (below) for Ban Na Dee, Viangthong District; many of them are still intact.

Lao Close Encounters

Cattle take advantage of fresh pasture provided by already-harvested rice fields at the base of a limestone massif (left) in Khamkeut District in October; another massif overlooks newly transplanted fields in June (below center). Even at Lak Sao, Khamkeut's District center, a massif overlooks the market square (second left). Lak Sao has an attractive and well-guarded temple (third left and bottom center). Mystery solved: why is this town named Lak Sao, i.e. Kilometer 20, when it doesn't seem to be 20 kilometers away from anything in particular? The answer lies in this sign (bottom left) east of town, placed by tourism authorities, at a tribal village named Ban Thong Bae. Although there is apparently nothing left to see from the former French presence, yet Lak Sao is 20 kilometers from this village, hence the name. There is even a Lak Sip Village (Kilometer 10) halfway between. Closer to the Vietnam border and still on Route 8, the Nam Phao River banks recently needed to be shored up to prevent erosion of the roadbed (below first right). Nam Phao is an official international border crossing, and this is the Lao border post (below second right). Just beyond is the Vietnam border post (bottom right), though the boundary stone announces "Lao" because it has been installed backward.

The Provinces   153

Champasak Province. A case could easily be made that this province (its name often spelled with a double s) has it all: falls of the Mekong plus many others in the interior, mountains and the cooler Boloven Plateau with its coffee, a 3-country corner, forests (vanishing) and dolphins (also vanishing), 4000 islands, an unusual colonial engineering solution, ancient religious monuments and an interesting formerly royal town, and most places are accessible even in the rainy season.

This Pakse building (top left) is currently a hotel, though it had been ordered built by Prince Boun Oum Na Champasak for his residence. The south was a separate principality until he renounced it in 1946. The view from the top of the hotel at the rear is of the Se Don River (top right), which soon enters the Mekong and gives the town its straightforward name (*pak se* means river mouth in southern Lao dialect). From the front of the hotel there is a panorama of the town's southeastern area, with the Mekong beyond (above). On the way up to the Boloven Plateau, blacksmiths in Bachiangcharoensouk District pound war scrap into machetes (left): note that the anvil is a shell casing. Hydrangeas and other ornamentals (right) grow well in the cooler Boloven climate in Paksong.

Lao Close Encounters

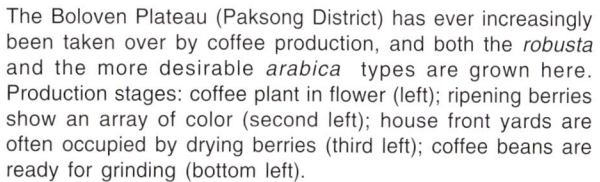

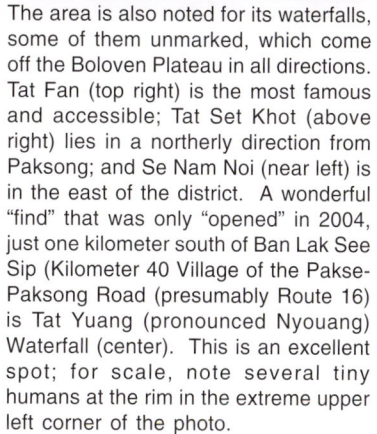

The Boloven Plateau (Paksong District) has ever increasingly been taken over by coffee production, and both the *robusta* and the more desirable *arabica* types are grown here. Production stages: coffee plant in flower (left); ripening berries show an array of color (second left); house front yards are often occupied by drying berries (third left); coffee beans are ready for grinding (bottom left).

The area is also noted for its waterfalls, some of them unmarked, which come off the Boloven Plateau in all directions. Tat Fan (top right) is the most famous and accessible; Tat Set Khot (above right) lies in a northerly direction from Paksong; and Se Nam Noi (near left) is in the east of the district. A wonderful "find" that was only "opened" in 2004, just one kilometer south of Ban Lak See Sip (Kilometer 40 Village of the Pakse-Paksong Road (presumably Route 16) is Tat Yuang (pronounced Nyouang) Waterfall (center). This is an excellent spot; for scale, note several tiny humans at the rim in the extreme upper left corner of the photo.

The Provinces

The famous Wat Phou, in Champasak District and now a UNESCO World Heritage site, is a Hindu Khmer temple complex predating Angkor. The lower level has the better preserved, though slightly less ancient, structures (above left and far left center). An overview of the lower level (above) shows the symbolic water reservoirs; the building in the center distance was Prince Boun Oum's Wat Phou residence, now removed. The uppermost level shows the wonder of the stonemasons' durable art, including Nagas (near left) and a female deity (below). The most ancient structure may be the crumbling portion behind the monk (bottom left); the central portion now houses incongruous Buddha images; the tiny spring that may be responsible for the complex's placement is off to the rear left.

Lao Close Encounters

In the ancient times this area was a great seat of civilization named Sethapura, becoming known in the 17th Century as Champanakhon (Vientiane Times, 4 May 2004), and subsequently as Champasak. Only a bit more recent than the oldest part of Wat Phou is a small outlier named Oum Muang or Oum Tomo (top left), also with some exquisite stonework such as this stela (center left) lying on the ground, near the east bank of the Mekong River in Pathoumphon District. Not ancient, but Mekong River oriented, this Buddha statue downriver from Champasak town is crowded by its flanking "*Bo*" trees (*Ficus religiosa*) (left); the associated temple has been "claimed" by the river.

Ferries are still in demand in the Si Phan Don (4000 Island) area, and pontoons are being welded for a new one (top right) in Pathoumphon District. The Mekong River (second right) appears placid in the late afternoon at the Champasak ferry crossing. In the 4000 Islands area, Khong District, the river spreads so widely that it becomes shallow, and channel markers (third right) are needed to show the way for navigation above the falls. Below the falls at the last village in Laos, Veunkham (bottom right), all is calm again. Everything beyond and to the right is Cambodia, and this an international border crossing both by water and nearby by land for those with visas in hand.

The Provinces   157

The great falls of the Mekong River, in Khong District, rank very high among the falls of the world in terms of volume of water, though not in terms of height. The falls are intersected by a string of islands. One of the easiest and most dramatic portions of the falls to observe is Khon Pha Pheng, seen from the eastern bank of the river (above left). The vantage point is operated as a park, containing a very useful map (above right) that shows the falls sectors, the islands, the international border, and even the spot preferred by the dolphins. Another portion of the falls (left) can be seen at the west side of Don Khon Island.

Difficult problem, clever solution: the French colonials, wishing to move goods up and down the river, were confronted by the falls. In order to circumvent the obstacle they built a 7-kilometer rail line from the bottom of one island below the falls (Don Khon) to the upper part of an adjoining island above the falls (Don Det), and accomplished their purpose. One of the locomotives (center) is preserved on Don Khon; portions of track (left) can also still be seen there, being used as pedestrian bridges across gullies. The top of the rail line on Don Det has a trestle (center right). The two islands (Khong District) are connected by a substantial railroad bridge (below center); a village bus crossing it has a nose simulating a locomotive. The bottom of the line on Don Khon has a large dock (below right) with a central inclined plane and winches to raise heavy cargo up to the railway level. The line is said to have been built in 1921 and abandoned in 1947. The last Lao engineer living at the southern end of the line in Ban Hang Khon village died in 2000.

Lao Close Encounters

Villagers who live close to the Mekong have ample water all year around, but "interior" villages have a problem in the dry season. Here in Set Nam Om village, Khong District, there is a nighttime waiting line for precious water gently retrieved from a pit dug more than 4 meters deep into a stream bottom down to bedrock (above left). Route 13 South ends suddenly beyond the Veunkham turnoff, but a forest track eventually comes to the border post and then the boundary monument more than 4 meters high announcing "CAMBODGE" (below left). The reverse of this monument announces "LAOS" (above center). Logging proceeds rapidly (above right) in western Mounlapamok District, where the lowland dipterocarp forest makes easy pickings. The western tip of Mounlapamok District is a 3-country corner, which officials have recently dubbed the "Emerald Triangle" (and which also refers to broad cooperation in tourist development among the three countries). It is extremely difficult to reach from the Lao side, but the Thais already advertise the spot as a tourist attraction on maps and signs (center right), and have built a 3-winged structure there named "Hearts Together Pavilion." A pedestal (near right) stands at the precise junction, with Thailand in the foreground, Laos at rear left and Cambodia at rear right. The pavilion is shown here (far right) from the Lao angle. Vung Tao (Phonthong District) to Chong Mek, Thailand, is a convenient international border crossing.

The Provinces

159

Houa Phan Province. This northeastern province, closest to Hanoi, has several important claims to fame. It straddles the Annamite Mountain Range, with part of its drainage going west into the Mekong River but the great majority of it going eastward to the Gulf of Tonkin. This mountainous terrain with little accessibility by people is good for wildlife. There is the mystery of the standing stones, called menhirs. It is widely acknowledged that the best cloth weaving comes from this province. A few ethnic tribes still wear traditional dress. Temple architecture is unusual. Last but not least, this is the province where the communist revolution against the monarchy and its American allies was planned, where a town was once intended (but not perpetrated) as the new capital of the revolutionary country, where there are monuments of victory and solidarity with the Vietnamese allies in struggle, and to where the King and Queen were banished and died.

The provincial capital of Sam Neua has a nearby hill that provides an overview of most of the town (above). A Vietnamese revolutionary monument (far left) stands atop another hill overlooking town. The Sam Neua market has some fine examples of the province's excellent decorative weavings (below left), but they can also be bought in Vientiane, now including a desirable shorter length of about 1.5 meters (center). There is a pleasant waterfall along the road southwest of Sam Neua (right), and fine scenery all over, including Viangsai District to the east (below).

Lao Close Encounters

The town of Viangsai was planned from the ground up after the end of hostilities in 1975, and since it was intended as the revolutionaries' new capital for the whole country (symbolically next to Vietnam and distant from Thailand), its few buildings are widespread around scenery like this pond (above left) and the revolutionary monument (above right). Needless to say, bomb casings abound (center left); and the revolutionary statue, incorporating both a hammer and a sickle, has a farmer, soldier, and laborer with a "USA" bomb underfoot.

Individual caves in Viangsai used during the revolutionary struggle include those of Kaysone Phomvihane, Souphanouvong (left), Khamtay Siphandone, and Nouhak Phoumsavan, and can be visited as a guided tour.

The Nam Sam River, here shown in southeastern Viangsai District (center right), gives its name to the towns of Sam Neua and Sam Tai (northern and southern Sam). This portion of the province is part of the Nam Sam National Protected Area (right).

The Provinces

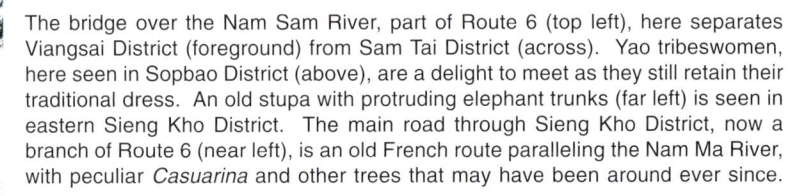

The bridge over the Nam Sam River, part of Route 6 (top left), here separates Viangsai District (foreground) from Sam Tai District (across). Yao tribeswomen, here seen in Sopbao District (above), are a delight to meet as they still retain their traditional dress. An old stupa with protruding elephant trunks (far left) is seen in eastern Sieng Kho District. The main road through Sieng Kho District, now a branch of Route 6 (near left), is an old French route paralleling the Nam Ma River, with peculiar *Casuarina* and other trees that may have been around ever since.

Sieng Kho town has weavers young and old who are still using natural dyes (above left). In Sieng Kho, even the filling station owner, who helps to drain the last drops out of the hose, is well dressed (above right). There is a scenic suspension walking bridge over the Nam Ma River west of Sieng Kho (left).

Lao Close Encounters

An old temple and stupa at Muang Et (top left), Et District, stand the test of time. In Houa Muang District, there is the ancient mystery of the menhirs (sign, center left), the standing stones (*hin tang*) up to 2.7 meters tall (above) that perhaps had a funereal function. A local man in the village with the menhirs, now in his nineties (above right) was on hand to assist a French archaeologist in the 1930s with her investigation. Three passing tribeswomen (left) stand atop one of the horizontal stone members (covering a hole) at Suan Hin Tang. In Viangthong District, eternal mountains and misty valleys (below) characterize the country, and a Yao boy (right) wears a traditional embroidered jacket as everyday clothing.

The Provinces

Khammouan Province. The southern part of this province is the beginning of the country's south, as shown by the Lao words for river. In the north of the province, there is the *Nam* Hin Boun, while in its south there is the *Se* Bang Fai. The province's capital is Tha Khaek, "guest landing," an indication of its history. There is a revered stupa; mining of gold and tin; a stone forest; the beauty and power (literally) of the Hin Boun area; incredible karst topography, with bluffs both precarious and substantial; and a mountain that you can pass under. The province's eastern area is among the least accessible in the country, good for wildlife, but another dam is in its preliminary stages, and this could make it easy for loggers and hunters. Tha Khaek to Nakorn Phanom is an international border crossing.

The Tha Khaek riverbank wall (top left) is a good place to sit and discuss the passing scene. French Indochinese architecture (top right) can be seen in all such provincial river towns. A famous old stupa, That Sikhotthabong (left), is on the Mekong River southward from Tha Khaek. Village revelers in the area celebrate a festival (below left). Route 12 eastward from Tha Khaek heads into magnificent karst topography (above); and columns of limestone in Mahasai District (below right) look as precarious as a stack of children's building blocks.

Lao Close Encounters

A river ford on a side road east of Tha Khaek comes unexpectedly with a depth gauge (left).
The stone forest of Phou Pha Man (right) is in the border area between the Provinces of Khammouan and Bolikhamsai.

Tin mining still occurs at Phon Thieu village, Hin Boun District, with the mine headquarters (above left) making it clear that it dates from the French. Other nations still make extractions from the area. Tailings wash down from the site of mining activity (above right). In Phi Pheng village, the façade of an old building (left), said to be a former tin storage depository while the product waited for purchase and transshipment by distant buyers, is still standing. Village men return from a boat race on the Hin Boun River (below left). The Hin Boun valley (below right) is a very pleasant area.

The Provinces

The Kong Lo—Natan Cave extends for 7.5 kilometers from Hin Boun District to Nakai District, providing the visitor with the unique experience of actually passing under a mountain from one side to the other by boat. Although undoubtedly the local people have been using this passage for centuries, it was officially "opened" as a natural tourism site in January 2002 amid fanfare including the printing of vehicle decals (above center). Since then it has had few visitors due to rainy season inaccessibility, but a proper road is on the drawing board. A pirogue is hired on the Hin Boun side at a pleasant park with a pond (above left); the cave is the small black hole at the rear. A boatman (above right) will not only see you safely through the journey, he may also teach you how to roll your own cigarettes. The boat enters the cave mouth (center left), but once inside there are various times, at least in the dry season, when it must be pushed and prodded over shallow sections (below left), and a one-way trip may take up to 1½ hours. Along the way there are interesting stalactites and stalagmites (below right), and a picnic ground at the Nakai end.

Lao Close Encounters

The upper reach of the Hin Boun River (above left) is the gateway to the Kong Lo—Natan Cave. Roadside waterfalls, such as this one (above) along Route 8 in Hin Boun District, are attractions of rainy season travel. Mahasai, with its temple shown here (above right), is a riverine town in the interior, giving its name to the surrounding District. A flood once washed out the cable of the Mahasai vehicular ferry on the Se Bangfai River, making it non-functional for a while (center right), but note the helpful transportation waiting for boat passengers on the other side. Vertical pale limestone bluffs (left) are awe-inspiring in Nyommalat District. This roadbed (below right) may be designated as Route 1 in Saibouathong District, and used by logging trucks and others during the dry season, but in the rainy season it is just the bottom of another rice field.

The Provinces

167

Luang Nam Tha Province. This province, also spelled Louang Namtha, is the second most northerly in the country and perhaps also the second most "tribal," at least for the time being. That flavor may change when the A3 Road is completed for traffic from Thailand to China. The agriculturally and geopolitically desirable Muang Sing area has had various suzerains and owners through the ages, making for some fascinating history. The province has mines, including copper and coal. The Mekong River first "kisses" Laos here, and the province is the birthplace of eco-tourism in the country. Boten to Mohan, China, is an international border crossing.

The town of Luang Nam Tha is in two parts, broadly separated by the greater airport area. While the northern part is the commercial seat, the southern part, shown here, is more interesting to explore. The town's temple is well adorned with murals (above right). The Nam Tha River was formerly the principal communication artery for the area, and the boat landing here (above left, upstream, and above right, downstream) continues to do business. The area abounds with ethnic tribes in original attire, such as the woman (below left) mixing cloth dye, and the one (below center) preparing yarn. The walking paths are good, including a village footbridge (below right) also being used for drying of newly dyed cloth. Patches of forest along the way are actually village burial grounds with amazingly ornate gravesites (right).

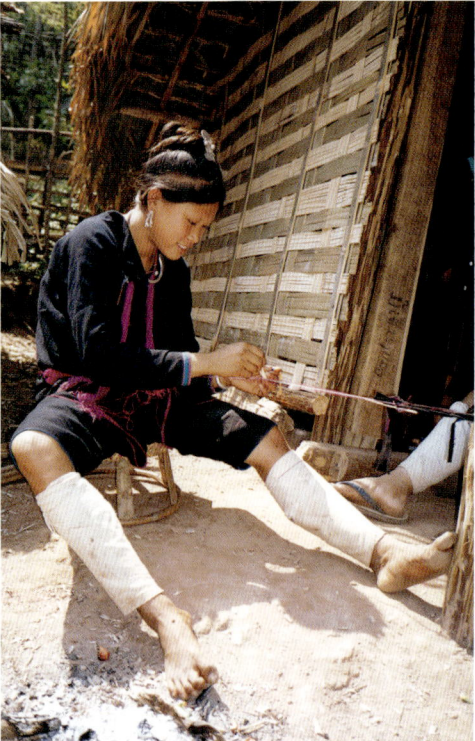

A significant portion of the province is within the Nam Ha National Protected Area, as announced by a sign in Viangphukha District (above); note that the "NPA" is an over-stencil from the former "NBCA," National Biodiversity and Conservation Area, which may have been regarded as too unwieldy. The Nam Tha River (above right), here seen along the road to Nale District, runs along part of the east side of the NPA. International travelers to China pass through the Boten checkpoint (right) in Luang Nam Tha District. Coal is extracted from an open pit mine (below right) in Viangphukha District along Route 3 not far above the Bokeo Province line. The night life in Viangphukha District is strained yet unrestrained (below).

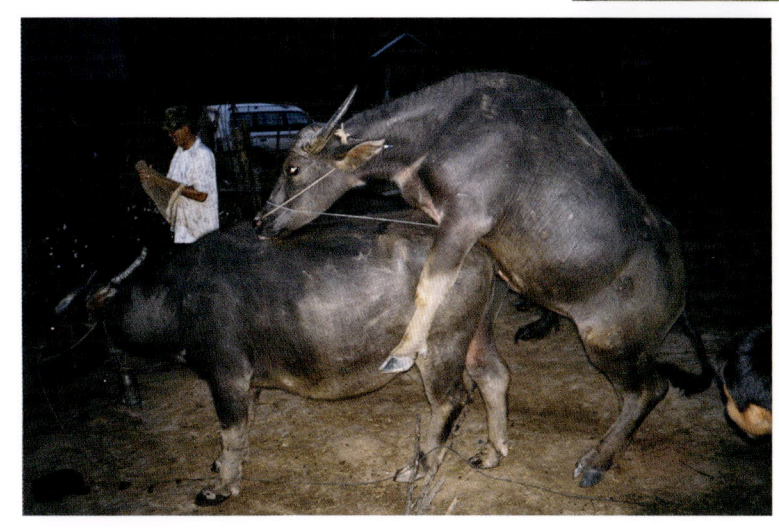

The Provinces

There is a pleasant waterfall with sunshades outside of Luang Nam Tha (above). This signboard greets the traveler on Route 17 entering Long District (above right), showing the ethnic diversity of the area. Route 17 ends at Sieng Kok, Long District, on a sharp bend of the Mekong River across from Burma, where there is a border checkpoint (center right). This is an offloading point for goods from China (below right), which arrive on Chinese boats and are transported inland on Chinese trucks. This fine old wooden village temple (below) is along the road from Luang Nam Tha to Oudomsai; it has no separate bell tower, but the drum and gong inside (left) are entirely functional.

Lao Close Encounters

The Muang Sing museum (left) is in downtown Sing; if you can find the custodian to let you in, the admission charge is minimal. The outdoor fresh market is a parade of tribespeople in traditional costume (above right and center right). Entrepreneurial tribeswomen sell woven cloth at their own row of stands (below center). The indoor market does have its lulls; if a particular stall has anything you wish to buy, just awaken the proprietress gently (bottom right). Some tribal villages in the area, such as this one near the China border northeast of Sing (below left), have spirit gates next to both entries to their community; this gate is next to the rear entrance.

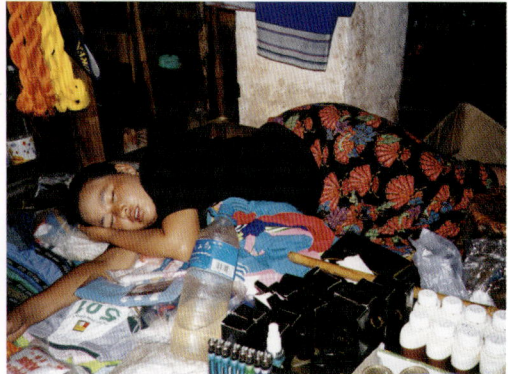

The Provinces

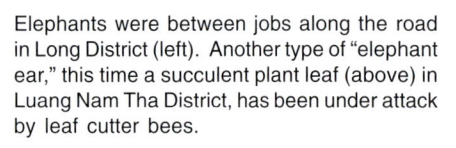

Elephants were between jobs along the road in Long District (left). Another type of "elephant ear," this time a succulent plant leaf (above) in Luang Nam Tha District, has been under attack by leaf cutter bees.

Although mountain tracks like this one northwest of Sing (left) are usually used only by walking or cycling tribesmen, it is remarkable how far they can sometimes be followed by 4-wheel-drive vehicles, including to mountaintops with dazzling views of sun-dappled hills beyond (above).

Another Sing District road goes almost to the top of the province, to the Houa Khong (head of the Mekong) checkpoint (top right), just 3 kilometers below the China border where the river first touches Laos. At this point, before any contribution to its volume from Lao rivers, it cannot be recognized as the same waterway that passes through the Si Phan Don area of the south: looking upstream from the checkpoint (second right) and looking downstream (third right); Burma across. Whirlpools in the river are also evident here (right); river photos taken in early May.

Luang Prabang Province. Luang Prabang, or Louang Phabang, is famous as the former royal capital and UNESCO World Heritage town, but it is also a large mountainous province that extends from Vientiane Province in its south to the Vietnam border in its northeast. It is now easy to get there, but the tourist load on Luang Prabang takes its toll. Of course it is no longer the same as it was years ago, but it's still a charmer.

In Sieng Ngeun District, an outlook over the northward descent of Route 13N into the Khan River valley (above) shows snippets of roadbed in a number of places. Those curves should not be taken too fast, however, as one never knows what is waiting around the next one (top right), Phoukhoun District. The new road along the north side of the Nam Suang River through Pak Seng District (second right) is picture perfect. Old temples like the one in Pak Seng District, with lions guarding (third right), are always a pleasure to encounter. Appreciation of the simple pleasures, like seeing rivulets fall over moss (below center), comes easy in Pak Seng District. Viangkham District has a forest track running northeast through it toward Vietnam, but as with many such roads in the rainy season, there comes a point when only 2-wheeled vehicles or pedestrians can go farther (bottom right). Villagers may overcome riverine obstacles with locally made footbridges like the one in Nambak District (below left).

The Provinces 173

Another excellent old village temple (left) is located on the east side of the Nam Ou River across from Nong Khiaw, Ngoi District. From Nong Khiaw, a boat is required to go upriver (right) to old Muang Ngoi. The old town is a very sleepy place, with little happening even on the main street (below right). The river, although it is the real thoroughfare, may not have much going on along it either (bottom left), as it is no longer as important as it was before the road to Phongsali was completed. However, it is a fine place for contemplation and for trekking, with which locals would be happy to provide some help (center left).

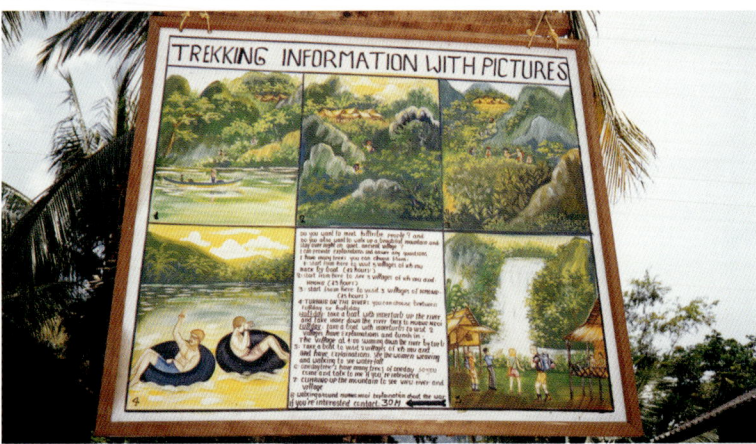

Lao Close Encounters

Leaving the ample bombie casings behind in old Muang Ngoi (center left), one can strike out for a walk in various directions. An eastward trail begins by passing right through the school grounds (above left), upon which a young woman with a well-worn English-Lao dictionary in front of her (above right) may charge you a small trail fee. Along the trail there is an interesting cave (center). In front of it there is a rock in the cave stream which a Western visitor found perfect for contemplation, while tribeswomen pass behind her (bottom left). Further eastward along Route 1 in Ngoi District are the caves used by the revolutionaries as their center of operations for the greater Luang Prabang area (below right). They have been furnished with stairs to provide access for visitors.

The Provinces

The Tham Ting (Pak Ou) caves contain myriad Buddha images (above left) and have historically been a pilgrimage site. The caves (below left) are in Chomphet District but are right across the Mekong River from Ban Pak Ou village, Pak Ou District, and the mouth of the Nam Ou River (bottom right). They can be reached in about 1½ hours by slow boat (above right), though you are not likely to be able to sit as still as the boat driver for that long. Along the way you may stop at the local filling station which is on another boat (center right), and to stretch and shop at villages making cloth, mulberry paper, and rice whiskey. The caves are a stop on the 2-day houseboat trip from Ban Houai Sai (houseboats below left). Speedboats (bottom right) may be used, but they utterly shatter the tranquility of the scene. Ban Pak Ou can also be reached in about 1 hour by road.

Lao Close Encounters

Ban Phanom village is about 4 kilometers eastward from downtown Luang Prabang and is fun to visit because the village showroom is so well stocked with cloth (above left and back cover) and because you can walk around the village and see lots of weaving in progress. Beyond is Henri Mouhot's tomb (below left) on a high bank of the Nam Khan River, near where he died. Mouhot was the Frenchman who rediscovered Angkor (seat of the ancient Khmer empire) for the Western world. He was a naturalist and explorer in an era when the term really meant something, and he survived everything but malaria. He kept meticulous journals, and was writing as he was dying, with the line from his pen ultimately trailing down the page. His home town of Montbeliard has installed a tribute at his tomb, indicating that it is "fière de son enfant." Further beyond in the same direction is Wat Sieng Lom (above center), including scenes of Buddhist monuments in various countries. Khouang Si Waterfall (above right) and its pleasant grounds are about 35 kilometers by road down the Mekong from Luang Prabang. While still a beautiful spot and well worth visiting, as a result of a collapse some years ago the falls is no longer the marvel of limestone depositional cones portrayed in older photos. The watercourse can be followed downstream for a distance, along which the deposited limestone creates smaller falls (right) and "individual" swimming holes. The water's heavy lime burden gives rise to unusual water coloration (below right). The grounds here contain tiger (below center) and bear enclosures.

The Provinces

Luang Prabang town is strategically located at the confluence of the Nam Khan River with the Mekong (center left). It is a very old town, dating from the 14th century, and was earlier called Muang Swa. The airport (top left) has made it easy to reach, now with nonstop flights from Bangkok and Chiang Mai in addition to Vientiane. Architecture such as that seen along the main street (above right), considered to be of Chinese style, is in part what has made the town worthy of World Heritage designation. The best overview of the town can be had by climbing Mount Phousi, with the downtown area visible upstream along the Mekong (below left). Another part of town can be seen from a slight angle downstream (below right); since Luang Prabang has over 30 temples, one or more of them is almost sure to be in any overview photo, in this case Wat Mai.

The former Royal Palace, built in the first decade of the 20th century, is now simply called the Luang Prabang Museum. Currently quite sparsely furnished, some pieces must have been dispersed; the deeply carved and inlaid set (below) may have been part of it, and this was used at a Vientiane venue for all to sit on until it was put away. Mount Phousi is just across the street from the Museum (below left). Privately held antiques like this urn (below center) are also no longer on display. That Makmo, the "Watermelon Stupa" (below right) on the south side of town near the Nam Khan River, is formally called That Prathoum.

The Provinces

179

There are two special things to do at night in Luang Prabang. One is to patronize the night market, which occupies a portion of the main street (below left). It is remarkable how quickly all of it can be put away if it begins sprinkling rain. Luang Prabang's weavers are well represented, though all of the hanging pieces behind this vendor (above left) are distinctly the handiwork of the famous Houa Phan Province weavers. On a chilly February evening, there is nothing wrong with the vendor wrapping up in one of the pieces she is hoping to sell (above center). The second thing to do at night is to attend a theatre performance of the Phralak-Phralam, the Lao version of the Ramayana. The theatre has been recommenced after a very long hiatus, and a few of the participants were actually in the pre-revolutionary troupe. The theatre sign (right) tells its own story about official policy. Picture taking is welcome at the finale of the indoor performance (below right), upon which the show moves outdoors for a segment from the Phou Noi (above right), an ethnic group from Phongsali Province.

Lao Close Encounters

Oudomsai Province. This province, also spelled Udomsay or with other permutations, has no National Protected Areas, though there are forested mountains and game is sometimes seen being sold along the road. Instead, it is better known for its agricultural and commercial sectors. Its crops are diverse, and rubber is playing an increasing role. Commercially, it is the crossroads capital of the whole northwest, the hub of 4 provinces, and with the new border crossing to China at Meochai its future is bright. The Chinese influence is strong. The Mekong River forms the southern border of the province, and Pakbeng is the overnight stop on the slow boat ride from Ban Houai Sai to Luang Prabang.

A good sized fish from the Mekong is on offer (above left) at a restaurant in Pakbeng, Pakbeng District. Unenviable passengers in a speedboat (above center) pass by Pakbeng in a rainstorm during their downriver hurtle; Sayabouli Province is across. River travel seems much more pleasant in the dry season. A half-arch of limestone (above right) at a public park in Namo District somehow manages to hold itself up. Children at a village in Nga District are fascinated with the outside mirror of a vehicle (below left), including the distortions reflected from the convex metallic front-facing surface. The new Meochai commercial vehicle crossing to China is in northern Namo District (below right), though it is not certain exactly when one has reached the border because the boundary monuments are on the hilltops and not on the road as yet.

The Provinces

Oudomsai is a boomtown with continuous new construction. The best overviews are to be had from atop Mount Phou Sai, here showing the downtown area (below) and toward the airport (above). The main feature of the mount, and for that matter of the whole town, is a large, well-maintained stupa (above right) that figures prominently in the spiritual life of the town.

Lao Close Encounters

There is also a dormitory for monks on the mount, and two novices take advantage of the presence of a checkers table (above left). There are occasions during the year when there is a procession of the faithful three times around the stupa, led by the monks (above right). The townspeople follow (below left). Small private rituals or observances may take place afterward (below right).

The Provinces

Phongsali Province. This is the country's most northerly province, and covers the upper reaches of the Ou River. Its remoteness has enabled it to retain its exotic character, and it is here that ethnic tribal life is perhaps the least changed. The roads are few, though two of them go into China and one into Vietnam. The French defended it during the colonial period, and that appears to have bearing on its being part of Laos today, though only about 10 kilometers (as the crow flies) east of the provincial boundary is the site where General Vo Nguyen Giap defeated General Henri Navarre at Dien Bien Phu (Theng), which led to the demise of the French in Indochina. There has been talk of opening the border so that international travelers may reach the battleground, but it does not seem to have happened yet. Roads here are mostly built and maintained by a Chinese labor force, and this seems to be reflected in the generous portion sizes in restaurants.

Route 2 meets the Nam Ou River at the town of Muang Khoua (top left) as seen from the east bank; a clever suspension bridge over the Nam Pak River at Khoua (center left) is adequate for light farm vehicles; a villager's art adorns a house (below left); all Khoua District. Another bridge near Muang Mai is just for foot traffic (above); the Lao border post at the eastern end of Route 2 is completely rural (below), making it hard to believe that Dien Bien Phu is only about 25 kilometers farther on; both Mai District.

Lao Close Encounters

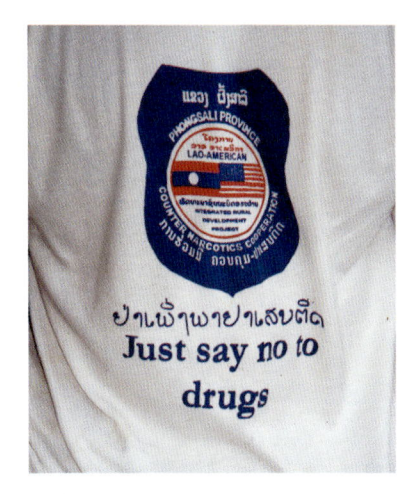

Parts of the French fort at Boun Tai still stand (above left), now used for administrative offices. The Americans assist the Lao from here in developing crop substitution methods and rural road construction (center left and left). There is a salt extraction site in the district on a hillside below a mineral hot spring (above right). The scenery includes valley floors of rice fields with villages nestled beyond (center right), and mountain peaks sticking out from cloud shrouded valleys (right). All Boun Tai District.

The Provinces

Red bell peppers are drying all over in April (above left); an Akha woman and her baby are on their way to the clinic (right); take your pick of fresh-killed squirrels or perhaps something already barbecued (left); all Boun Tai District. An overview of the terrain near the boundary between Boun Tai and Samphan Districts (below) can be seen from the American-built road. These hybrid Chinese vehicles, half-tractor and half-truck (below left), are popular in the northernmost provinces; Boun Neua District.

Lao Close Encounters

The water buffaloes "claim" the traffic circle in Boun Neua (above left); tribeswomen adopt similar poses (left) while waiting for a vehicle to pass by; the China border at the southwestern end of Route 19 is well marked with a 2-faced boundary monument (top right); all Boun Neua District. The name of this village is Home (right), but not for many; Ou Tai has a magnificent old slate-roofed temple (below left), and the interior wooden structure required to hold up all that stone (below right) is an architectural and artistic marvel by itself; all Nyot Ou District.

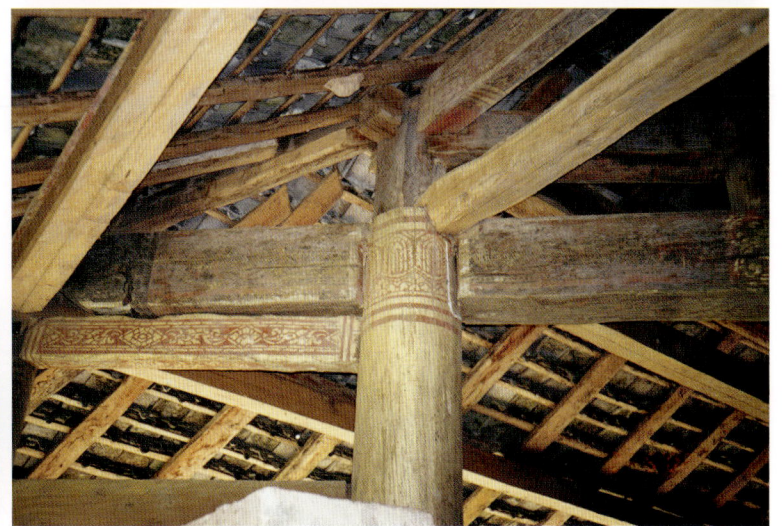

The Provinces

The boat landing at Hatsa village (left), northeast of Phongsali on the Nam Ou River, long ago was the best way to get near the provincial capital even though it is some 20 kilometers away by road; and although its role has diminished it is still important for local travel. Slash-and-burn agriculture in the area can be quite intense (above left). The frontier image of Phongsali town is reinforced by a herd of horses galloping by (above). Phongsali is ringed with mountains (below) and is subject to being "socked in" by morning fog. All Phongsali District.

Saisomboun Special Zone. This area, also spelled Xaysomboun, was created out of parts of several provinces in 1994 and given a military administration in order to prevent insurgent activity. Several years ago two districts, Longsan and Hom, were returned to Vientiane Province, leaving only the three districts of Phoun, Saisomboun, and Thathom strung along Route 5, with Saisomboun town about 100 kilometers eastward from Route 13N. While there seem to be no official roadblocks to travel in the Zone, yet landslides, incomplete construction, and local advice do limit movement. The Zone is home to the highest mountain in the country, Phou Bia at 2819 meters, which can be approached by a road northward from Saisomboun but landslides will prevent going forward, and the mountain seems shrouded in mist all the time. Saisomboun District also contains Sam Thong and Long Cheng, the famous "Alternate" of the Vietnam War era, where General Vang Pao and his Hmong army held forth along with the Ravens, American pilots of the "secret war" in the northern area. The road from Route 5 northward through Long Cheng, and on to Phasai in Sieng Khouang Province, seems perfectly good, though friendly advice at both ends of the line was "better not go." Official denial of alleged recent military atrocities against the Hmong in the area appeared in the Vientiane Times as lately as 4 October 2004, where it was concluded that reports in the foreign press were slander by bad elements.

The strength of an elephant to move logs even through stony forest (top left) should not be underestimated; tribal people choose high ground for their houses and granaries (top right); bulldozers have a schedule for maintaining roads, unless their trailer drivers take a curve too sharply (above); all Phoun District. Route 5 crosses the Nam Ngoum River valley (center right), the boundary between Phoun and Saisomboun Districts. Beginning at the sign (below center), the road northward to Long Cheng is very good about 20 km up (bottom right); Saisomboun District.

The Provinces

Promises, promises: in Saisomboun Special Zone, the road construction company puts up the signboards first and then builds the roads later. In this one (below) it shows a 120-kilometer shortcut to Route 13S, which they are working on. In another (bottom right) it shows a 49-kilometer road to the highest mountain, and indeed you can ascend the track for some distance, with scenery like this (bottom center) before a landslide turns you around.

The scenery along Route 5 eastward from Saisomboun town inspires awe (top left), until the road turns into a buffalo wallow (top right); however this can be driven around, and eventually the road reaches a crest and begins its long descent into the valley of the Nam Ngiap River (center), Thathom District.

The expansive and the earthy: Saisomboun means "abundant victory," a grandiose name, while the name of a village on the east side of town, Ban Khi Sang (above), means elephant feces village. Saisomboun can be viewed from various angles, including northward from the hotel veranda (top right), southward to "downtown" from the hotel (center), and eastward toward town from a temple along the road on a misty morning (bottom left). The market square and bus depot (bottom right) is the center of activity. The hotel's front porch pillars are nicely carved (top left).

The Provinces 191

Salavan Province. The claims-to-fame of this province (also spelled Saravane) are the Tat Lo Waterfalls on a stream descending from the Boloven Plateau, its ethnic diversity which is more apparent in village architecture than in dress, and the fact that it is the third-most UXO-contaminated province in the country. Salavan town, the capital of the province, is in the interior and not very photogenic. The province is served by Route 15 from Route 13S to the Vietnam border, however its three northeastern districts are much more easily reached through Thapangthong District in Savannakhet Province due to the difficulty of getting across to the north bank of the Se Don River. Remote Samouay has recently begun to receive electricity from Vietnam. The province has some accessible National Protected Areas.

The lower falls at Tat Lo (center left) are very pleasant, while the upper falls (top) are spectacular. The main ethnic group in the area is the Alak, who may have villages with a large common ground (above) and a meeting hall with icons at the gables, such as this one with a helicopter icon (left). All Lao Ngam District, off Route 20.

Lao Close Encounters

Getting around other stuck vehicles (above) is only one of the problems of interior travel; the scenery is "gentle" (above right); both Toumlan District. There is not much happening in "downtown" Ta-Oy (center left); one boy has a striped squirrel (*Tamiops*) for sale, while the other smokes a cheroot (right); cattle ford the Se Lanong River (bottom left); all Ta-Oy District.

The Provinces

The theme of gently rounded scenery continues here (above left), not the straight or jagged peaks of Khammouan Province northward; the Lalai border post (above right) is near the northeast end of Route 15; this tribal village (center left) was momentarily evacuated because the UXO squad was exploding bombs in the vicinity, and note that the village is fenced from large livestock to help keep it clean; rice granary legs are exclusively cluster bomb casings (center right); the design of a tribal village meeting hall (bottom right) is precise; all Samouay District. Curious buffaloes swim over to check out the big white thing stuck in their river (bottom left), the Se Don northwest of Salavan next to the bombed out bridge.

Lao Close Encounters

Savannakhet Province. The superlatives about this province are many, though not the usual ones. They have to do with size (one of the largest provinces), population (the most populous province), city rank (Savannakhet is the second largest), and economic potential. On the other hand, it is probably also the flattest province, and thus perhaps the least awesome, least ethnic, and most easily exploited. Another superlative is that it is one of the two most unexploded ordnance-contaminated province as a result of its situation across from the Vietnam War's Demilitarized Zone at the 17th Parallel, with the center of the Ho Chi Minh Trail passing through its eastern districts. One ethnic group represented here is the Phouthai, who moved into the upper Se Banghiang valley from what is now northwestern Vietnam many centuries ago. Some of them have moved to Savannakhet town and have become commercially successful in naturally dyed textiles for export. Several parts of National Protected Areas are easily accessible, including the Dong Phou Viang NPA south of Phin. The province's economic future is bright, with gold and copper mining, the Route 9 reconstruction completed in 2004, the Savannakhet-Mukdahan bridge (financed by Japan) over the Mekong to be finished in 2006, with a corresponding special economic zone, and a potential seaport provision for Laos at Dong Ha in Vietnam. Although few photos of mining are shown anywhere herein, mineral extractions actually take place in many of the provinces, covering gold, copper, coal, lead, zinc, barite, lime, and salt (Vientiane Times, 29 November 2004). Savannakhet's Sepon District currently has the lion's share of gold and copper production. Both ends of Route 9, Savannakhet-Mukdahan and Daensawan-Lao Bao, are international border crossings.

The morning mist has yet to lift over the rice fields (above); waterfalls are a pleasant sight in Dong Phou Viang NPA (top right); tall trees grace a side road in the same NPA (left); and a Vietnamese-built revolutionary statue stands in "downtown" Phin (second right); all Phin District. Copper mining begins (third right) in Vilabouli District. This restaurant family holds forth in Sepon town (below). The border at Daensawan is actually a small stream; you can tell where Vietnam starts by the red-topped posts (bottom right), Sepon District.

The Provinces

The scenery of Savannakhet is mostly low and rounded, and often with fragile soils subject to erosion when the tree cover is removed; resistant caprocks occasionally remain over the top of a tower of earth in a highly eroded area (above); along one watercourse there is a spillway accommodating a roadbed below it in early May when it is still the dry season (below left), while in late August at the same spot the situation is quite different (below); all Thapangthong District. Villagers of Ban Bouk Thong in Champhon District make water urns (left) from local clay, currently retailing at 4000 kip (US 40 cents).

Lao Close Encounters

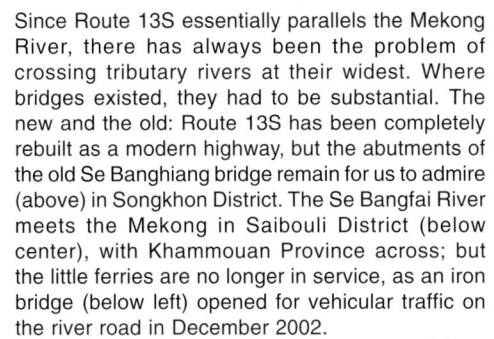

Since Route 13S essentially parallels the Mekong River, there has always been the problem of crossing tributary rivers at their widest. Where bridges existed, they had to be substantial. The new and the old: Route 13S has been completely rebuilt as a modern highway, but the abutments of the old Se Banghiang bridge remain for us to admire (above) in Songkhon District. The Se Bangfai River meets the Mekong in Saibouli District (below center), with Khammouan Province across; but the little ferries are no longer in service, as an iron bridge (below left) opened for vehicular traffic on the river road in December 2002.

Heuan Hin ("Stone House," top right) is a pre-Angkor Khmer shrine in Saiphouthong District on the Mekong southeast of Savannakhet. Apparently related is this unpublicized monument ruin (center) surrounded by fields in neighboring but non-riverine Champhon District, close to the rainy season house of this family (below right), here posing for a semi-formal portrait. That Phon stupa, (center right), a revered Hindu monument of uncertain age, is not far from Heuan Hin in Saiphouthong District. Encountering things for which there seem to be little or no explanation, such as this crumbling brick structure (top center) in Sonbouli District, is part of the allure of the countryside.

The Provinces

The Savannakhet immigration and customs house is on the Mekong River waterfront (top left). Lao passenger ferries and cargo boats load at the Mukdahan landing on the Thai side (top right), Savannakhet across. The new Japan-sponsored bridge, as seen under construction from the Lao side at Savannakhet in March 2005 (above), to be completed in December 2006, will have a profound impact on trade. High quality cotton yarn is prepared by ethnic Phouthai for the next step as vats of indigo dye stand by (left); natural ingredients are boiled for a range of color dyes (right) in Savannakhet.

Lao Close Encounters

Sayabouli Province. The name of this province probably has more spelling permutations than any other, ranging from Sayaburi to Xaignabouly. There are only two stretches where the west bank of the Mekong River is part of Laos; most (but not all) of the northern stretch is in Sayabouli. The west bank changed hands several times during its modern history, ultimately in French hands and thus part of Laos today. Instead of the Mekong, the boundary follows the tiny Nam Heuang River in the extreme south and then the watershed up into Bokeo Province in the north. This makes it more difficult to be precise, and indeed this is the country's only land border that is not yet totally physically demarcated. This gave rise to a shooting argument between the two countries in 1987-88 in Boten District, when the two were apparently following different map versions as to where the border should be. The province has an elongated upside-down L shape today, though formerly the string of its four northern districts were part of Oudomsai, and you may see some maps that still show it that way. It has a rather unique set of circumstances that are favorable for its prosperity. The soil is fertile for upland crops, there is no UXO contamination and large tractors are able to be used for some cultivation, agricultural and material trade with Thailand are close at hand, and river travel also makes year-round commerce easier. There is not yet any official entry point for third country international travelers, but the new Nam Heuang River bridge at Kenthao, completed in October 2004, could make this a reality in the future.

The usual way to enter the province is through Nan District of Luang Prabang Province, taking the ferry across the Mekong (top left) to the west bank (right side of photo) in Sayabouli District. The country has a one-Party system, though there was an election of sorts in 2002; what better place to look at the particulars of the candidates than waiting for the Sayabouli ferry (center left)? In the former Kingdom of a Million Elephants, Sayabouli probably has more than any other province, whether they are walking to the next logging job, or working as part of a road improvement "chain gang" team (above right) in Sayabouli District, or training as entertainers (below right) in Pak Lai District. There are currently said to be over 1000 wild and 800 domesticated elephants in the country (Vientiane Times, 11 April 2003); as for the location of wild populations, the Nam Poui NPA (below left) is mentioned first; Phiang District.

The Provinces

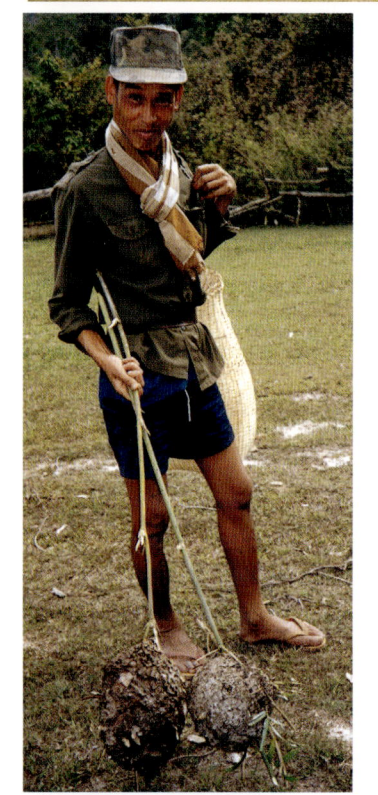

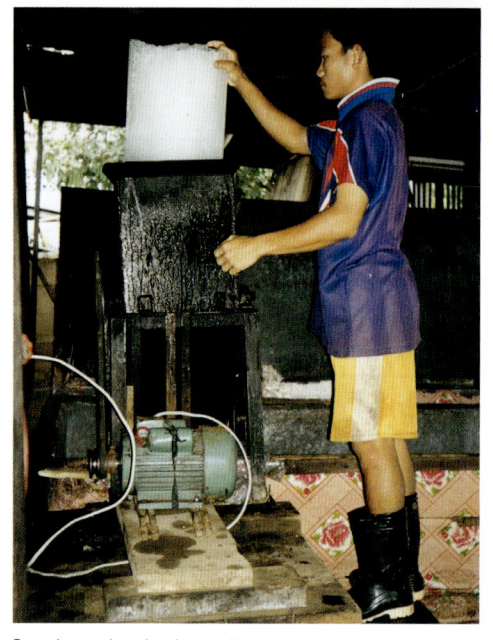

Good grazing in there, but the school grounds may not be the best place for cattle (top left); harvested logs have smaller diameters than in some other provinces (top right); both Phiang District. A forest gatherer shows his harvest of ant nests (center left); Thongmisai District. The ice man satisfies the needs of local trade (center); *posa* (mulberry bark strips) is in much demand, including from the Thais (center right); the Mekong River boat landing (below right) is the center of activity in Pak Lai; best loo view in all of Asia: whether due to river flood damage or to renovation, this Pak Lai toilet has been left with a breathtaking view to contemplate; all Pak Lai District.

While the occasional bullock cart may still be in use along Route 4 (above left), Western farm tractors can also be seen (above right); Kenthao/Boten District. The Nam Heuang River in Kenthao District (center left) is not many boat lengths across to Tha Li District, Thailand, but it has since become the site of a new international bridge. The same river in Boten District (center right) is even narrower to Na Haeo District, Thailand, in the dry season. New and old: a new pavilion for a reclining Buddha (bottom left) is in Kenthao District, and a fine old temple (bottom right) is in Boten District.

The Provinces

There are some good stretches of hill forest along the northern road (top left); sometimes there is a choice between the high road and the low road to get across a stream (top center); a nicely color-coordinated village woman adjusts her head strap to carry home a load of grass for making brooms (second left); a mountain village house maximizes its drying space (third left); how could the butterflies be any "friendlier" than this (bottom left)?; very interesting old temples are found here and there (above); temple altars are photogenic (top right); murals on the temple façades tell stories (right); all Hongsa District.

There is a good, all-weather road from the town of Ngeun to the Thai border at Nan Province, so it should not be surprising that trade here is oriented to Thailand. The sign (top left) faces people coming from Thailand, while the one (top right) welcomes people to the district from the provincial town; both Ngeun District. From Ngeun to Sienghon District, there are portions of the road where snippets of what is to come can be seen from all angles (center left), while other portions are relatively straight (center right); an old temple with an effective but incongruous new roof (bottom left) can be seen on the way. Sizable herds of cattle (bottom right) are seen in some villages in Sienghon District.

The Provinces

203

Sienghon is also a welcoming place (left), with prosperity indicated by some brick houses and flowering plants (right). From Sienghon to Khop District, the theme of historic temples (center left) and photogenic altars (bottom left) comes up again; the main road here often looks like a private driveway with its grass strip down the center (bottom center). "Downtown" Muang Khop (center right) is scenic if not populous. The boat landing at the northeastern border of Khop District (bottom right) is a minor but busy stop on the Mekong, Bokeo Province across.

Lao Close Encounters

Sekong Province. This is named after the Se Kong River, which has its headwaters in the northern part of the province and which flows past the capital and on to Attapeu Province and into Cambodia. It is also the headwaters of the Se Kaman River. There are only four districts, with the western two (Lamam and Thateng) reached easily enough, but the other two (Kalum and Dakchung) among the remotest districts in the entire country. It may be appropriate to consider the province to be the least populous, the least visited, the least Buddhist, and with the least published information of all. The high percentage of tribal people surely makes it an anthropological wonderland. And, once again, we are right back on the Ho Chi Minh Trail.

Looking up the beautiful Se Kong River at the provincial capital is a reflective experience (above). The main landmark of the provincial town is the hotel (above right). The arrival of a traveling salesman provides a little excitement to village life (right), Thateng District. The word "Se Kong" spray-painted by a road crew on a downed tree (below right) is the only way to know that one has arrived in Kalum District after a tortuous trip northward from the provincial capital on a track that crosses into Salavan for a stretch. Lao women have the remarkable ability to bathe fully clothed and then change their entire outfit in public while completely preserving their modesty, some steps of which are seen here (below) on the banks of the Se Nam Noi River in Lamam District.

The Provinces

205

The Se Nam Noi River tumbles in stages off the highlands of the Boloven Plateau at rear, this stage called Tat Faek Waterfall (above left and above right) just before it enters the Se Kong River; on the way eastward on Route 16 toward Dakchung, groups of village houses may be surrounded by a wall of scavenged cluster bomb casings (below left); all Lamam District. Bomb craters capture rainfall and allow tree growth in an otherwise dry upland (bottom left); a tribal village maintains an immaculate common area (bottom right); and children haul poles home from the forest (center right); all Dakchung District.

Lao Close Encounters

The terrain becomes rugged in the uplands between the Se Kong and the Se Kaman drainage basins (above); a roadside forest market features "bush meat" and tubers (above left), while a mother hopes to sell citrus to passersby (center left); villagers warm themselves in a January morning mist in "downtown" Dakchung (below); a 122 millimeter cannon (bottom left) along the track southward toward Sansai in Attapeu is a reminder that this is part of the Ho Chi Minh Trail; a forest burial site along the same track (bottom) includes whatever may be needed, including radio, utensils, fuel, clothing and money, and a scraped but living tree in the same area (center) has the details of one departed individual's life; all Dakchung District.

The Provinces

207

Sieng Khouang Province. This province, also spelled Xiangkhoang, was once larger than it is now because the three districts remaining in the Saisomboun Special Zone were carved out of it. A large part of it is a high, rolling plateau that can remain chilly even into early March. Pine forests still abound in the mountains, and agar wood (*Aquilaria*), highly desired as a perfume in the Arab world, is cultivated and harvested here. Although the province has no National Protected Area, yet its eastern districts are quite pristine and remote, with remarkably clean mountain streams. It is most famous for its Plain of Jars (*thong hai hin*), so named because of the clusters of huge carved stone jars crafted and scattered around it by a civilization that lived there up to 3000 years ago. Despite its antiquity and its beauty, the province has a great sadness about it because it was so thoroughly devastated during the Vietnam War. This area was not part of the main Ho Chi Minh Trail to the south, but its contested strategic location resulted in the devastation being particularly severe, especially since it tended to change hands along with the changes of the season. The objective of the West was the interruption of the indigenous communist movement, but in the attempt to deprive the combatants of resources, the civilian population experienced great suffering. Old timers here, including the older tour guides, can provide firsthand accounts to visitors about how their own families suffered. The intensity of the bombing here is said to be second only to that in Savannakhet Province, and the unexploded ordnance (UXO) problem is huge, with seven people recently killed in one episode alone (Vientiane Times, 19 October 2004). The provincial capital of Ponsawan, also known as Muang Pek, is a new, planned community.

Ordnance as decoration is nowhere more frequently used than in Ponsawan, and simply making a tour of the displays in hotel and guest house lobbies is an education in itself (top right, above left and above right). One of the most popular restaurants in Ponsawan has a nightly showing of the remarkable television documentary "Bombies", by Jack Silberman, Lumiere Productions Inc., with firsthand accounts of the bombing and of the unexploded ordnance problem then and now. A war monument built by Vietnam at Ponsawan shows the military solidarity of the two countries (below left). The open air Ponsawan "wet" market is a colorful place (below center), but is being replaced by a two-story building. Ponsawan has a broad layout that makes it seem rather sparse (below right).

Lao Close Encounters

The once-proud provincial capital, Sieng Khouang town, was so thoroughly bombed that almost nothing was left standing, and the new village that is there today is named Muang Khoun, a district headquarters. This is the most intact of the prewar buildings (above left), and this is what remains of the ancient Wat Phiawat (above right). An old stupa still stands upright (left), but is peculiarly hollowed (right), apparently not by bombs but by fortune hunters. A local family in Phasai District "hangs out" on a North Vietnamese Army tank that is a leftover of war in front of their house (below left); it appears to be the remains of a Russian T76 tank. A metal scrap yard in Pek District contains largely war-related materials (below right).

The Provinces

Tragic day: a pilot made a direct hit on Tham Piew Cave in Kham District, where many families had taken shelter from the bombing, and all inside lost their lives (above left). A memorial to those who died there has recently been erected (above right), with an inscription (above center). Buddhist artwork appears in a cave in the vicinity of old Muang Soui, Phoukhout District, that was used by Neutralist Colonel Kong Le in the first half of the 1970s (right). A ripening rice crop in Kham District shows how productive the area can be, with a view of the rolling plateau (below). Family members bring in the corn crop in Nong Het District as the bull looks on (below right).

210   Lao Close Encounters

Plain of Jars site 1 (top center) in Pek District is well marked along the road south from Ponsawan (top left). Site 1 has a large bomb crater (occupying the entire foreground of the photo), with the series of jars adjacent to it damaged (above). Jars site 2 in Phasai District is a more comfortable, leafy place (center left); unfortunately some of those leaves are on a tree that has been allowed to grow inside a jar, thus damaging it (top right). Jars site 3, in Phasai District, is also leafy (bottom left). Sites 1, 2, and 3 are together expected to achieve World Heritage listing in 2006, and to this end, site 1 was officially cleared of UXO in 2004 and the other two are underway (Vientiane Times, 20 & 21 October 2004). There are up to 50 jars sites in the province, the remainder less frequently or rarely visited; at this one, the guide points out clay Buddha images that he found inside a jar (right center). Pleasant waterfalls in Phasai District are a short drive from jars sites 2 and 3 (bottom right).

The Provinces

Parts of Khoun District are flat, but its south and southwest are mountainous (left). Rock blasting is in progress in Khoun District to help clear the track toward Mok Mai (above center). Mok Mai District is arguably the most remote in the entire country; its mountain track is seen here (above right). A Mok Mai District stream runs clean and clear, passing by tree ferns (bottom left). Route 7 in Nong Het District climbs into the clouds heading for Vietnam (center). A hot spring in Kham District has a pipe capable of providing warm baths (below right). A hill tribe clings to the roadside along a ridgeline in Phoukhout District (bottom right).

Lao Close Encounters

Vientiane Province. Although this province has the same name as the capital city and the Capital territory, it is a separate administrative entity. It is headquartered at Viangkham, north on Route 10 and on the bank of the Nam Ngoum River. There is French colonial architecture in the town, but unlike other provincial seats which are clearly the hubs of activity for their respective areas, Viangkham calls little attention to itself, especially since it is located on a byway. The spelling of the word "Vientiane" is a convention; if the Lao pronunciation were to be more accurately transliterated, it would resemble "Wiang Jahn." (Convention and pronunciation are often at odds, helping to explain why there is not yet any reasonable standardization of place name spellings.) Longsan District and Hom District were quietly returned to Vientiane Province several years ago from their temporary placement in Saisomboun Special Zone though the government's year 2000 administrative map has not had an updated printing. The easiest road access to both of these districts is by way of the south entrance to the Phou Khao Khouai National Protected Area, beginning in Thaphabat District of Bolikhamsai Province. Vientiane Province can be seen as highly desirable by the tourist in that it is so beautiful, with so may recreational opportunities, and yet so close to the Capital. In only three or four days, one could see Thoulakhom District's Zoo, and National Protected Area (assuming the dry season); Keo-Oudom's Nam Ngoum Reservoir; and participate in Vang Vieng's river sports or caving.

Fuang District is accessed by taking the road west from Hin Heup, just before the Nam Lik bridge. It has spectacular scenery, with limestone karst rising at right angles from rice fields (above); its minorities may be identified by their architecture, such as this Thai Dam house (top), and no longer by clothing. The road continues to Sanakham District, a long journey since Route 11 up the Mekong River from Vientiane is not complete. Students return home for lunchtime in "downtown" Sanakham (below); and an elephant trudges along the river road northeast of town (below right), after loading logs onto boats headed for the Capital. Met District is reached in the dry season by a road heading southwest from an angle in Route 13N south of Muang Kasi, but the road is so long that some local people find it easier to meet their marketing needs by taking a boat down the Met River (right) to its junction with the Mekong.

The Provinces

The picturesque Longsan valley, here with its compound for hydroelectric staff (below left), is seen from the high ground of the northern limit of Phou Khao Khouai NPA. Muang Hom is difficult to locate and very small, but it does have a "pump" (filling station) (center) that unexpectedly shows itself as being affiliated with an international oil company. Viangkham District still has its funky ferry on the Nam Ngoum River (center left), but hurry up: bridge plans have already been announced. Heading up Route 13N, you know that you have reached Hin Heup when you arrive at the one-lane iron bridge over the Nam Lik (top left). Students head home in Phonhong District along Route 13N (top right), an area prosperous from its extensive fertile, flat rice fields and proximity to markets. Keo-Oudom District contains most of the Nam Ngoum Reservoir; the village perched rather precariously on its bank (above) just above the dam has good restaurants. From this village very slow boats may be hired for rides around the reservoir's islands, some of them inhabited (below).

Thoulakhom District is the western gate to Phou Khao Khouai NPA. In the dry season, the plateau with its pine forests and villages can be visited, including the river (top left) beyond Ban Wang Heua. The district is also home to the zoo, with its northern Lao white elephant (below right), the only known white male in the country and highly respected among Buddhists. The "Paya Xay Ya Mongkun" shown on the zoo ticket (above center) is the elephant's name. The renaming of the zoo as "Lao Zoo" creates something of an unintended double entendre with Lao Tzu, the ancient Chinese philosopher. Exotic animals also await the zoo visitor, such as this Australian ostrich (above right). Africa and the Middle East are also represented by hippopotamus and camel (above and below); both L. Swanson photos.

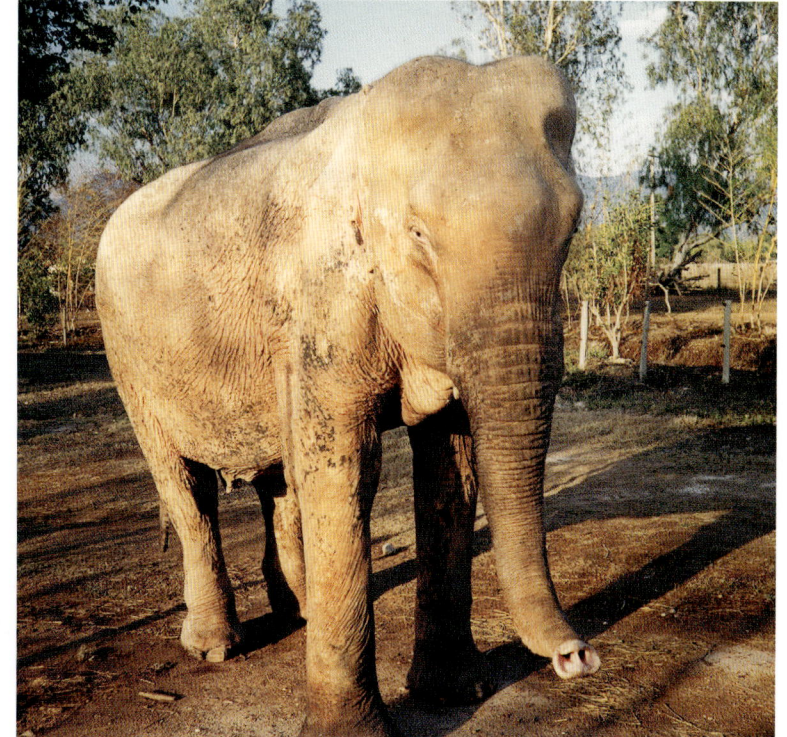

The Provinces

Kasi District is remarkably photogenic. No matter how often one passes by the mountain massif northeast of town, it seems that its moods require more photos. For example, compare September (above left) with the same angle in November (left), and at a different and more distant perspective (below left). A karst hill overhangs Route 13N at one point (right); and ripe rice straw stacks like those of Phoukhout District, Sieng Khouang, may be seen in Kasi (below). The long dry season road southwest toward Met District has some tree ferns along the way (above).

Vang Vieng District and its town have long been popular with tourists. Boat races marking the end of Buddhist Lent in October are held here on the Nam Sang River (above). Souvenir shops are ample (above right), now including a new market complex, and the locals are used to being photographed (below). The caves and some of the best walking and biking are across the river, which is crossed by hiring a boat (left) until the dry season walking toll bridge is put back in place (third right); larger vehicles just ford the river (bottom right). Some of the menu boards in town are in Hebrew (right). At one point a while ago, Route 13N was threatened by an adjoining stream (below left); drivers must stay alert everywhere.

The Provinces

217

Those going tubing on the river go four kilometers upstream from Vang Vieng by *tuk-tuk* (above), may need to cross a sandbar in the dry season (below), and down they go (bottom right). Kayaks are loaded (above left) to begin farther upstream, and kayakers get a briefing (center left) before launch. The endpoint for everyone is a landing at the lower end of town, here shown with local maidens in the foreground having their evening river bath (bottom left).

Lao Close Encounters

CONCLUSION

The traffic sign (above left), seen in Mounlapamok District of Champasak Province, seems to sum up the ambivalence of the country: there may be some voices and some circumstances that favor keeping the brakes on, but it can't be done because even the stop sign is green. May the country's leaders show great wisdom in development planning and the management of issues attendant upon a rapidly expanding population, with a view to preserving natural resources and ethnic diversity for many generations to come. Champasak District bids you have a good trip, and so do I.

If a photo show is supposed to end with a sunset, here it is (left), taken along the bank of the Mekong River just downstream from Vientiane in August. But in this case, it may be more appropriate to conclude with a rainbow (below), taken in Phou Khao Khouai National Protected Area in Bolikhamsai Province, because Laos is the "pot of gold" at the end of it.

Conclusion

INDEX

Adenium obesum 98
Aerobics 44
Agar wood 86, 208
AGRICULTURE AND FORESTRY 67-100
Aid Donors 30
Airline fleet 116
Akha ethnic group 186
Alak ethnic group 192
Alms 31, 60, 61
Alocasia macrorhizos 131
Alpinia malaccensis 132
Alternate 189
Aluminum boats 117, 151
American legacy 25-29, 36, 208, 210
American program sponsorship 29, 185
Americans missing-in-action (MIA) 29
Animals 82-85, 136-143
Annamite Mountains 126, 143, 160
Anousawali 11
Appias lyncida 138
Appias nero 138
Aquaculture 72
Aquilaria 86, 208
Arc de Triomphe 11
Arctonyx collaris 142
Army of the Republic of Vietnam (ARVN) 26
Artists 115
Arundinaria graminifolia 131
ASEAN Summit 116
Asian Development Bank 23, 123
Association of Southeast Asian Nations (ASEAN) 1, 3, 12
Attapeu 28, 43, 145-146
Attapeu Province 26, 28, 43, 87, 91, 118, 127, 138, **144-146**
August 23 Park 14
Australia aid donations 30, 122
Avian (bird) flu 85, 144
Awk Phansaa 58
Babies 39
Bachiangcharoensouk District (Champasak) 79, 86, 101, 154
Baci (basi) 42
Badger 142
Badminton 46
Baguettes 23, 53
Bamboo 101, 102, 103
Bamboo water pipes 65
Bamboo, Rattan, Wickerwork 103
Ban Dong 26, 28
Ban Hang Khon 158
Ban Houai Sai 22, 147-148, 176, 181
Ban Khi Sang 191
Ban Lak See Sip 155
Ban Na Dee 152
Ban Nongheo 103
Ban Pak Ou 176
Ban Phanom 104, 108, 109, 177
Ban Sieng Lom 105
Ban Sop Ruak 149
Ban Thong Bae 153
Bananas 79
Bang fai phayanak 150
Banknotes 6
Barbecued food 50, 51
Bats 141
Bauhinia 134

Bauhinia variegata 133
Baw Kaew 147
Beer 112
Bees 137, 172
Beetles 137
Bell peppers (capsicum) 78, 186
Bells 33
Beng District (Oudomsai) 141-142
Betel nut 76
Bicycles 9, 113
Biodiversity 87
Bird flu 85, 144
Birds 140
Blacksmiths 154
Blessing with water 54, 55
Bo trees 157
Boards 102
Boat builder 105
Boat racing festival 58, 217
Boats 105, 117-118, 148-149, 152, 166, 174, 176, 181, 198, 200-201, 204
Bokeo Province 67-68, 124, 130, **147-149**, 169, 199, 204
Bolikhamsai Province 1, 2, 7, 8, 32, 43, 50, 67-69, 72, 74, 76, 83, 85, 97, 117, 126-129, 133-135, 138, 140-141, 143, **150-153**, 165, 219
Boloven Plateau 62, 75, 82, 110, 123, 154-155, 206
Bomb clearance 27, 194
Bombax ceiba 135
Bombies 27, 175, 208
Bombing of Laos 25, 208-209
Boten (Luang Nam Tha) 168-169
Boten District (Sayabouli) 199, 201
Bougainvillea 99
Boun Bang Fai 56-57
Boun Neua 187
Boun Neua District (Phongsali) 78, 186-187
Boun Phawed San Don 54
Boun Tai 185
Boun Tai District (Phongsali) 22, 185-186
Breakfast 53
Brickmaking 111
Bricks 111
Bridge construction 30, 118,145, 198
Bridges 3, 83, 120-122, 126, 145, 154, 158, 162, 173, 184, 197, 214, 217
Brooms 97, 202
Broussonetia papyrifera 93-95, 200
Brugmansia 99
Brunei 226
Bubalus bubalis iv, 46, 82, 169, 187, 190, cover
Buddha Park 2, 20
Buddha images 15, 20, 35-37, 148, 157, 176, 201
Buddhism 31-37
Buddhist flag 31
Buddhist monks 31, 34, 37, 59-61, 66, 183
Buddhist nuns 60
Buddhist relics 15
Buffalo Horn Mountain 150
Bugs 137
Burial grounds 22, 168, 207
Burls 104
Burma 147, 149, 170, 172, 226
Buses 3, 125
Butea monosperma 135
Butterflies 138, 202
Caddisflies 137

Calisthenics 44
Callosciurus 141
Cambodia 143, 226
Cambodian border 74, 144, 157, 159
Canines 51, 84
Capital Sights 9-16
Capital territory 9-21
Capsicum 78, 186
Carambola 81
Carp 72
Carpetmaking 107
Cassava 64, 77, 99
Cassia agnes 135
Cassia fistula 134
Castalius rosimon 138
Casuarina 162
Cattle 82, 125, 127, 153, 193, 200-201, 203
Caves 147, 161, 166, 175-176, 210, 217
Ceiba pentandra 96
Champanakhon 157
Champasak 39, 98, 157
Champasak District (Champasak) 46, 69, 70, 130, 156, 219
Champasak Province 2, 6, 8, 27, 39, 40, 42, 43, 46, 50, 62, 68, 70-76, 79, 82-83, 86, 88-89, 91, 96, 101, 110, 124-125, 128-131, 143, **154-159**, 219
Champhon District (Savannakhet) 55, 71, 113, 139, 197
Charcoal 89
Checkers 43, 183
Chiang Khong (Thailand) 147-148
Chiang Rai (Thailand) 149
Chiang Saen (Thailand) 148-149
Chickens 85
Children 39-40, 46, 64, 83
Chillies 78
China 79, 119, 147, 168, 184
China border 78, 172, 181, 187
China trade 147, 170
Chinese investment 112
Chinese New Year 16
Chinese opera 47
Chinese pavilion 44
Chinese salesman 113
Chinese Temple 16
Chomphet District (Luang Prabang) 35, 176
Chong Mek (Thailand) 159
Christian churches 38
Citrus 79, 207
City wall 9
Civets 141
Classical dancing 14, 65, 180
Clay 111, 196
Clerodendrum paniculatum 132
Cloth weaving 108-109, 160, 176-177, end papers, back cover
Clothing factory 112
Cluster bombs 27, 28, 146, 161, 175, 194, 206
Coal mining 147, 169
Coconuts 79
Coffee production stages 155
Coffins 66
Coleoptera 137
Colonel Kong Le 210
Communism 24
CONCLUSION 219

220 Lao Close Encounters

Concrete building construction 102
Conservationists 136
Construction 101-102, 111
Copper mine 195
Coprinus disseminatus 130
Corn 76, 210
Corypha umbraculifera 133
Crabs 136
Cremation 66
Curcuma zedoaria 132
Currency 6
Curry 53
Cyathea chinensis 133
Cymbals 49
Daensawan 195
Dakchung 206-207
Dakchung District (Sekong) 26, 206-207
Darts 46
Death 66
Deer 142
Delonix regia 100, 134
Desert rose 98
Development assistance 30
Diamond Triangle 144
Dien Bien Phu (Vietnam) 22, 184
Dike 119
Dinner 53
Diptera 137
Dipterocarps 87, 159
Discover Laos 3
Distilling 106
Districts 1
Dogs 84
Dok so fa 35
Dolphins 143
Domestic air service 116
Domestic Animals 82-85
Don Chan Island 74-75, 82, 120-121
Don Chan Village 18
Don Det Island 96, 158
Don Khon Island 73, 158
Don Sao Island 149
Dong Amphan National Protected Area 87, 91, 138, 144
Dong Dok 19
Dong Ha (Vietnam) 195
Dong Phou Viang National Protected Area 195
Dorcus 137
Doughnuts 51
Dremomys rufigenis 141
Drought 119
Drug suppression 29, 81
Drums 33, 48, 49, 105
Ducks 85
Dust 124
Dyes, natural 108, 198
Electricity industry 7-8
Elephants 4, 21, 83, 88, 127, 172, 189, 199, 213, 215
Emerald Triangle 159
End of Buddhist Lent 58
English-language periodicals 3
Entertainment 47-49
Eriocaulon sexangulare 130
Erosion 121, 148, 196
Et District (Houa Phan) 73, 163
Ethnic groups 62-65
Ethnic Handicrafts Center 11
Eucalyptus 86
Eurema simulatrix 138

Factories 112
Factory Hands 112
Farmers 75, 77
Fauna 136-143
Fences 82, 103
Ferries 2, 118, 145, 148, 151, 157, 167, 197-199, 214
Festivals 54-61
Ficus religiosa 157
Filling stations 129, 176, 214
Fire 17, 89, 90
Fish 51, 53, 181
Fish Farming and Fishing 72-74
Fishponds 99
Flags 12, 24, 31, 226
Flame trees 100
Flies 137
Flooding 119, 120
Flora 130-135
Foe (feu, fur, pho) 53
Food 50-53
Football 43
Forest 87
Forest harvested 88
Forestry Department 87
Fort Carnot 22
Fortune telling 47
Fountain Circle 9
Four Thousand Islands 157
France aid donations 30
French cemetery 22
French explorers 117, 177
French food 23
French forts 22, 153, 185
French Indochinese architecture 23, 164
French Legacy 22-23
French railway 122, 158
French trees 23
Fresh markets 10
Freshwater shrimp 52
Friendship Bridge 3, 122
Fruit 79-81
Fuang District (Vientiane) 29, 40, 213
Funeral procession 66
Fungal rot 89
Furniture 105
Game (wild) 136, 141-143
Gardens (horticultural) 98
Geese 85
Gekko gecko 139
Gem mines 147
General Henri Navarre 184
General Vang Pao 189
General Vo Nguyen Giap 184
Generators 8
Germany aid donations 30
Giant water bugs 52
Glutinous rice 50, 53, 68, 71
Goats 83
Gold jewelry 4, 114
Golden Triangle 144, 149
Goldsmiths 114
Gongs 49
Government development programs 8, 87, 112
Grain extraction 70
Granaries 65, 189
Grapes 79
Grass 97
Grass roofing 101
Grinding devices 64

Guest houses 18
Guitar 49
Hammer-and-sickle 24, 161
Hatsa 7, 188
Hatsaifong District (Vientiane Capital) 36, 41, 72, 103, 106, 112, 122
Haw Phra Kaeo 15
Hemiptera 137
Henri Mouhot 177
Herbal remedies 10
Herbivorous animals 82
Heuan Hin 197
Hexagonia tenuis 130
Hin Boun District (Khammouan) 69, 83, 86, 127, 165-167
Hin Boun River 165, 167
Hin Heup 213
Hin Hoep District (Vientiane) 66, 139, 214
Hin tang 163
Hinkhanna Falls 21, 45
Hmong crafts 5
Hmong ethnic group 5, 62, 189
Ho Chi Minh Trail 25, 26, 27, 144, 195, 205, 207
Hom 214
Hom District (Vientiane) 91, 189, 213-214
Hongsa District (Sayabouli) 100, 202
Horses 82, 188
Horticulture 98-100, 154
Hotels 18, 24
Houa Khong (Bokeo) 147
Houa Khong checkpoint (Luang Nam Tha) 172
Houa Muang District (Houa Phan) 163
Houa Phan Province 46, 71, 73, 74, 77, 88, 109, 126-127, 130, 132, 138, 143, **160-163**, 180
Houai Sai District (Bokeo) 22, 67, 130, 147
Houn District (Oudomsai) 76
House fires 17
Hunters 141-143
Hydroelectric dams 7, 74
Hylopetes alboniger 141
Hymenoptera 137
Indonesia 226
Industry 112
Insect eating 52
Insects 136-138, 202
International air service 116
International border crossings 147, 153, 157, 159, 164, 168, 195
INTERNATIONAL HERITAGE 22-30
INTRODUCTION 1-8
Iron buffalo 67, 82
Irrawaddy dolphins 143
Islamic mosque 38
Jackfruits 80
Japan aid donations 30, 198
Jean-Renaud 23
Jewelers 114
Job's tears 77
Joint ventures 112
Jujubes 79
Jump rope 46
Kai ping 50
Kale 75
Kalum District (Sekong) 205
Kamphaeng Nakhon 9
Kampuchea 226
Kapok 96
Kasi District (Vientiane) 68, 78, 90, 97, 132, 216
Kayaks 218

Index 221

Kaysone Phomvihane 1
Kaysone Phomvihane Museum 19
Kenthao District (Sayabouli) 84, 201
Keo-Oudom District (Vientiane) 7, 72, 214
Khaen 48, 55, spine
Kham District (Sieng Khouang) 51, 78, 101, 126, 210, 212
Khamkeut District (Bolikhamsai) 7, 8, 43, 62, 67, 68, 69, 72, 74, 83, 97, 117, 126-127, 133-134, 153
Khammouan Province 24, 52, 69, 70, 83, 86, 127, 135, 141, 151, **164-167**, 197
Khanthabouli District (Savannakhet) 89
Khao lam 50
Khim 48
Khmer temples and monuments 156-157, 197
Khoa District (Phongsali) 7
Khon Pha Pheng Falls 158
Khong District (Champasak) 8, 43, 72-74, 96, 128, 143, 157-159
Khong Island 43
Khongwong 49
Khop 204
Khop District (Sayabouli) 65, 204
Khoua 184
Khoua District (Phongsali) 184
Khouangsi Waterfall 99, 143, 177
Khoun 209
Khoun District (Sieng Khouang) 64, 84, 125, 127, 135, 138, 142, 209, 212
Khuadin Market 10
Kian 100, 125
King Fa Ngoum statue 15
King Setthathirat statue 36, 61
King Sisavangvong statue 15
Kip 6
Kon Tum Province (Vietnam) 144
Kong 48
Kong Lo-Natan Cave 166-167
Kong phen 33
La District (Oudomsai) 41, 78, 131
Label on clothing 112
Lagerstroemia macrocarpa 134
Lai heua fai 58
Lak Sao 153
Lalai 194
Lamam District (Sekong) 139, 205-206
Lamwong 14, 44, 47
Lan Sang (Lan Xang) 83
Land of a Million Elephants 83, 199
Land use planning maps 152
Landscaping 14
Landslides 126, 173
Lanten ethnic group 109
Lanterns (paper) 94
Lanyaat 48
Lao Airlines 116
Lao Americans 36
Lao Aviation 116
Lao Bao (Vietnam) 195
Lao International Trade Exhibition & Convention Center (ITECC) 47
Lao National Museum 19, 24, 148
Lao New Year 54-55
Lao Ngam District (Salavan) 192
Lao People's Democratic Republic 1
Lao Railway Authority 122
Lao Trader 3
Lao Zoo 7, 140, 142-143, 215
Laongam District (Salavan) 55

Law and Order 6
Leeches 136
Legacy of War 25-29, 36
Lepidoptera 138
License plates 9, 29
LIFE 31-66
Limestone 151, 153, 164, 167, 177, 181, 213
Limestone forest 151, 165
Lion dance 16
Lizards 139
Log bridges 126, 202
Logging 88, 144, 159
Logs 88, 89, 102, 200
Long Cheng 189
Long District (Luang Nam Tha) 127, 170, 172
Longan 80
Longkong 79
Longsan District (Vientiane) 91, 118, 189, 213-214
Longsan River 214
Looms 108
Lorises 143
Lottery tickets 47
Lotus 80
Louang Namtha, see Luang Nam Tha
Louang Phabang, see Luang Prabang
Loven ethnic group 62
Luang Nam Tha 93, 102, 106, 109, 113, 117, 168, 170
Luang Nam Tha District (Luang Nam Tha) 169-170, 172
Luang Nam Tha Province 7, 22, 38, 57, 62, 63, 65, 109, 117, 127, 132, 140, **168-172**
Luang Prabang 4, 5, 32, 34, 42, 48, 49, 51, 53, 58, 62, 71, 75, 85, 93, 94, 99, 102, 104-106, 108, 109, 114, 117, 177-178, 180
Luang Prabang District (Luang Prabang) 131, 135
Luang Prabang Museum 179
Luang Prabang Province 2, 35, 62, 63, 64, 65, 77, 84, 86, 90, 91, 109, 113, 123, 125, 129, 131-132, 135, 143, **173-180**
Lunch 53
Lychees 79
Macaca mulatta 143
Maeng da 52
Mahasai 167
Mahasai District (Khammouan) 52, 164, 167
Mahogany 23
Mahosot Hospital 13, 23
Mai District (Phongsali) 184
Mak lawt 81
Mak leuay 77
Malaysia 226
Mangoes 79, 81
Mangosteens 79
Maps and Signs 1-2
Marigolds 98
Marx and Lenin 24
Mattresses 96
Meeting halls 146, 192, 194
Mekong River 30, 39, 72-75, 118, **119-121**, 148-150, 154, 157, 164, 170, 172, 176, 178, 181, 197-200, 204, 213, 219
Mekong River blasting 147
Mekong River Bridges 1, 3, 30, 122, 198
Mekong River Commission 13
Mekong River Falls 158
Melastoma malabathricum 131
Melons 79
Menhirs 160, 163, 226
Meochai border 181

Merit-making 31, 59
Met District (Vientiane) 68, 69, 213, 216
Metal detectors 28
Meung District (Bokeo) 147
Military 6, 7, 22
Milling rice 71
Mineral production 195
Mini markets 10
Ministry of Agriculture and Forestry 136
Mohan (China) 168
Mok Mai District (Sieng Khouang) 212
Monkeys 143
Monks 31, 34, 37, 59-61, 66, 183
Monument 11
Morning Market 2, 4, 11
Morus 92-93
Moscow 24
Motorbikes 9, 45
Mounlapamok District (Champasak) 42, 89, 91, 124, 159, 219
Mount Phou Sai (Oudomsai) 182
Mount Phousi (Luang Prabang) 178-179
Muang 1
Muang Boun Tai Fort 22, 185
Muang Et 163
Muang Khoun 209
Muang Pak Lai Fort 22
Muang Pek 208
Muang Sing 168
Muang Sing Fort 22
Muang Sing Museum 171
Muang Soui 210
Muang Swa 178
Mud 124-125, 190, 193
Mukdahan (Thailand) 195, 198
Mulberries 92
Mulberry Paper 93-95, 176, 200
Mun pao 75
Muntiacus muntjak 142
Murals 36
Museums 19
Music 48-49
Musical instruments 48-49
Myanmar 226
Na Haeo (Thailand) 201
Naemorhedus sumatraensis 142
Naga fireballs 150
Nagas 32, 58, 156
Nakai District (Khammouan) 166
Nale District (Luang Nam Tha) 169
Nam Bak District (Luang Prabang) 84
Nam Et National Protected Area 126, 138
Nam Et River 73
Nam Ha National Protected Area 169
Nam Heuang River 199, 201
Nam Khan River 75, 105, 117, 173, 177-178
Nam Lik River 213-214
Nam Ma River 162
Nam Met River 213
Nam Ngai River Dam 7
Nam Ngiap River 190
Nam Ngouang River 152
Nam Ngoum Reservoir 95, 214
Nam Ngoum River 21, 40, 118, 150, 213
Nam Ngoum River Dam 7, 118
Nam Ou River 174, 176, 184
Nam Pak River 184
Nam Phao 153
Nam Phao River 153

Nam Phao River works 7
Nam Poui National Protected Area 199
Nam Sam National Protected Area 161
Nam Sam River 161-162
Nam Sang River 217-218
Nam Suang River 173
Nam Tha 3 Dam 7
Nam Tha River 117, 168-169
Nam Thoen River 74, 117, 152
Nam Thoen River Dam 7
Nambak District (Luang Prabang) 113, 173
Namo District (Oudomsai) 76, 181
Nan District (Luang Prabang) 199
Nan Province (Thailand) 203
Nasaithong (Vientiane Capital) 56, 57
Nasaithong District (Vientiane Capital) 49, 67, 72, 130, 133
National Biodiversity and Conservation Areas (NBCA) 87, 136, 169
National Cultural Hall 13
National dance 44, 47
National flag 24
National Geographic Service 1
National Library 20, 23
National Museum 19, 24, 148
National Protected Areas (NPA) 87, 136, 169, also see named Areas
National University of Laos 19, 20
Natural history 1, 130-143
Natural resources 87
NATURE 130-143
Nelumbo nucifera 130
New Economic Mechanism 24
Nga District (Oudomsai) 181
Ngeun 203
Ngeun District (Sayabouli) 63, 87, 100, 109, 203
Ngoi District (Luang Prabang) 77, 174-175
Nok hong 4, 35, 37
Nong Het District (Sieng Khouang) 133, 210, 212
Nong Khai (Thailand) 3, 122
Nong Khiaw 174
Non-governmental organizations (NGO) 30, 136
Noodle soup 53
Nop 61
Normal Trade Relations (NTR) with U.S.A. 1, 29
North Vietnamese Army (NVA) 25, 209
NPA, see National Protected Area
Nycticebus coucang 143
Nycticebus pygmaeus 143
Nymphaea nouchali 131
Nyommalat District (Khammouan) 141, 167
Nyot Ou District (Phongsali) 22, 187
Old Muang Ngoi 174
Onions 146, 152
Operation Lamson 719 26
Opium 81, 147
Oracella brevirostris 143
Orchids 100
Ordnance as decoration 208
OTHER INTERESTING OCCUPATIONS 92-114
Ou Tai 187
Ou Tai fort 22
Oudomsai 57, 116, 182
Oudomsai Province 41, 57, 76, 78, 91, 131, 141-143, **181-183**
Oum Muang (Oum Tomo) 157
Outhoumphon District (Savannakhet) 100, 123
Oxcarts 100, 125, 201
Pa kha 143

Pa nil 51, 72
Paguma larvata 141
Paintings 115
Pak Kading District (Bolikhamsai) 50, 128-129, 135, 141, 143, 151
Pak Lai District (Sayabouli) 22, 96, 135, 139, 199-200
Pak Mong 42
Pak Ngum District (Vientiane Capital) 21
Pak Ou District (Luang Prabang) 176
Pak Seng District (Luang Prabang) 173
Pakbeng 181
Pakbeng District (Oudomsai) 181
Paksan 140
Paksan District (Bolikhamsai) 150
Pakse 74, 76, 86, 154
Pakse District (Champasak) 83
Paksong 154-155
Paksong District (Champasak) 27, 40, 50, 62, 75, 110, 131, 154-155
Pancakes 92
Panthera tigris 143, 177
Papayas 79
Paper (mulberry) 93-95
Park development programs 8, 14
Party flag 24
Pathoumphon District (Champasak) 39, 71, 74, 89, 125, 157
Patusai 11, 12
Patusai Park 14
Pavo muticus 140
Pavonia repanda 131
Peanuts 78
Pek District (Sieng Khouang) 70, 81-82, 111, 208-209, 211
Peppers (capsicum) 78, 186
Periodicals 3
Petanque 23, 43
Pha-Oudom District (Bokeo) 148
Phasai District (Sieng Khouang) 189, 209, 211
Phayanak 4
Phiang District (Sayabouli) 93, 95, 199-200
Philippines 226
Phin 195
Phin District (Savannakhet) 25, 28, 88, 113, 132, 141, 195
Phongsali 188
Phongsali District (Phongsali) 188
Phongsali Province 7, 22, 62, 63, 78, 180, **184-188**
Phonhong District (Vientiane) 36, 49, 53, 73, 214
Phonsai District (Luang Prabang) 86
Phonthong District (Champasak) 159
Phou Bia 189
Phou Khao Khouai National Protected Area 40, 49, 131, 138, 150, 213-215, 219
Phou Noi ethnic group 180
Phou Pha Man 165
Phou Phanang National Protected Area 133
Phou Sang He National Protected Area 88
Phoukhoun District (Luang Prabang) 2, 62, 64, 65, 113, 123, 129, 132, 173
Phoukhout District (Sieng Khouang) 123, 128, 133, 210, 212
Phoun District (Saisomboun) 70, 88, 90, 132, 189
Phouthai ethnic group 195, 198
Phouvong District (Attapeu) 127, 144-146
Phralak-Phralam 180
Pi Mai Lao 54, 55
Pigs 84
Pillar of Vientiane 35

Pillows 96
Pine forests 208
Pineapples 80
Pirogues 105, 117-118, 166, 168, 201, 204
Place mats 95
Plain of Jars 15, 27, 208, 211
Plants 130-135
Poinsettia 99
Police 6
Pomelo 79
Pong 33
Ponsawan 39, 52, 81, 114, 208, 211
Poppies 81
Population pressure 87
Posa 93-95, 200
Post Office 11
Post-Harvest Losses 65, **89**
Pottery 5, 196
Poverty reduction 90, 112
Power Generation 3, **7-8**
Presidential Palace 13
Primates 143
Prince Boun Oum Na Champasak 154, 156
PROVINCES 144-218
Rabbits 84
Radermachera ignea 134
Ramayana 180
Rambutans 80
Rats 52, 65, 141, 143
Rattan 103
Recreation 42-49
Red chilli peppers 78
Reforestation 86, 91
Relocation programs 90
Resin 89
Revolutionary monuments 19, 160-161, 195, 208
Revolutionary struggle 19, 160-161, 175
Rhizomys 141
Rice 50, 53, **67-71**, 82, 153, 185, 195, 210, 213, 216
Rice whiskey 106, 176
Right-of-way 128
River fords 124, 165, 194, 217
Road development 123
Road signs 2
Roads 123-129, also see Routes
Rock fall 127
Rocket Festival 56-57
Rodents 52, 65, 141, 143
Roofing 101
Route 1   25, 78, 125, 152, 167, 175, 211
Route 2   184
Route 3   147, 169
Route 4   201
Route 5   189-190
Route 6   162
Route 7   123, 212
Route 8   128, 151-153, 167
Route 9   123, 195
Route 10   213
Route 11   213
Route 12   164
Route 13 North   126, 173, 214, 216-217
Route 13 South   2, 55, 123, 128, 150, 159, 197
Route 15   192-194
Route 16   155, 206
Route 17   170
Route 18   87, 144
Route 19   78, 187
Route 20   192

Index

Royal Palace 34, 179
Runway upgrade 116
Russian Circus 24
Russian Legacy 24
Russian missile 146
Sai District (Oudomsai) 141-143
Saibouathong District (Khammouan) 70, 167
Saibouli District (Savannakhet) 197
Saiphouthong District (Savannakhet) 197
Saisettha District (Attapeu) 118, 145
Saisomboun 189-191
Saisomboun District (Saisomboun) 189-190
Saisomboun Special Zone 70, 86, 88, 90, 132, **189-191**, 206, 213
Salavan 25, 140, 192, 194
Salavan Province 25, 28, 55, 82, 139-140, **192-194**, 205
Salesmen 113
Salt extraction 185
Sam Neua 160-161
Sam Neua District (Houa Phan) 127, 132
Sam Tai 161
Sam Tai District (Houa Phan) 162
Sam Thong 189
Samouay 192
Samouay District (Salavan) 28, 82, 194
Samphan District (Phongsali) 186
Samsaenthai Road 16
Sanakham 213
Sanakham District (Vientiane) 126, 213
Sanamsai District (Attapeu) 87, 146
Sanasomboun District (Champasak) 125
Sandbar at Vientiane 119
Sangthong District (Vientiane Capital) 8, 21
Sansai District (Attapeu) 26, 87, 91, 138, 144, 146, 207
Sapphire mining 147
Saraca indica 135
Saravane, see Salavan
SARS 144
Savannakhet 38, 195, 198
Savannakhet Province 25, 26, 28, 31, 38, 55, 71, 84, 88-89, 100, 113, 123, 126, 129, 132, 137, 139, 141-142, **195-198**
Saw 48
Sawyers 102
Sayabouli District (Sayabouli) 199
Sayabouli Province 22, 63, 65, 70, 84-85, 87, 93, 95-96, 100-101, 109, 135, 139, 181, **199-204**
Sayo Laos 3
Scaffolding 102
Scavenging war scrap metal 27, 28
School 41
Se Bangfai River 167, 197
Se Banghiang River 25, 195, 197
Se Don River 25, 154, 192, 194
Se Kaman River 118, 145, 205
Se Kong River 145, 205-206
Se Lanong River 193
Se Nam Noi River 139, 205-206
Se Nam Noi Waterfall 155
Second Mekong River International Bridge 30, 198
Sekong 140, 205
Sekong Province 26, 43, 139-140, **205-207**
Senna alata 133
Sepak takraw 42
Sepon 195
Sepon District (Savannakhet) 26, 28, 141-142, 195
Serow 142

Serving spoons 53
Sesame seed 77
Sethapura 157
Seventeenth Parallel (Vietnam) 26
Si Phan Don 157
Sieng Kho 46, 162
Sieng Kho District (Houa Phan) 162
Sieng Khouang 209
Sieng Khouang Province 39, 51, 52, 64, 69, 70, 78, 81-82, 84-85, 101, 111, 114, 123, 125-128, 133, 135, 137-138, 140, 142, **208-212**
Sieng Kok 170
Sieng Ngeun District (Luang Prabang) 62, 125, 129, 173
Sienghon District (Sayabouli) 63, 65, 70, 87, 101, 203-204
Signs 2
Silk carpets 107
Silk thread 108
Silk, raw 92
Silkworms 108
Silver jewelry and bowls 4, 114
Silversmiths 114
Silviculture 86
Sing 140, 171
Sing District (Luang Nam Tha) 57, 63, 140, 168, 171-172
Singapore 226
Singing 49
Sinh 110
Skateboards 45
Slash-and-Burn 90-91, 188
Snakes 139
Soccer 43
Solar panels 8
Sonbouli District (Savannakhet) 129, 196
Songkhon District (Savannakhet) 197
Sopbao District (Houa Phan) 162
Soukhouma District (Champasak) 68, 76, 88, 129-131
Souvannakhom Kham 148
Souvenirs 4-5, 95
Soviets 24
Spiders 136
Spirit gates 38, 63,171
Spirit worship 38
Spiritual Matters 31-38
Squirrels 52, 141, 186, 193
Starfruit 81
State-owned enterprises 24
Stereum ostrea 130
Stick bridge 21
Sticky rice 50, 53, 68, 71
Stone forest 151, 165
Stone House 197
Street drainage 17, 124
Students 6, 9, 13, 17, 41, 110, 214
Stupas 15, 36, 57, 66, 150, 162-164, 179, 182, 197
Suan Hin Tang 163, 226
Sugar cane 76, 79
Supermarket 1, 10
Sweden aid donations 30
Sweet-and-sour 53
Swidden 90-91, 188
Swietenia mahagoni 23
Swine 84
Tabanus 137
Tagetes patula 98
Takaw 42

Tamiops 193
Tanks, military 26, 209
Ta-Oy 193
Ta-Oy District (Salavan) 139, 193
Tapioca 64, 77, 99
Tat Faek Waterfall 206
Tat Fan Waterfall 155
Tat Khouangsi Waterfall 99, 143, 177
Tat Leuk Waterfall 138, 150
Tat Lo Falls 55, 192
Tat Moon Falls 21, 44, 45, 124
Tat Sai Waterfall 150
Tat Set Khot Waterfall 155
Tat Yuang Waterfall 40, 155
Teak 86
Temples 31-35, 37, 153, 167-168, 170, 173-174, 177-178, 187, 201-204
Temporary island 120
Termites 89, 136
Tha Deua 3
Tha Khaek 164
Tha Khaek District (Khammouan) 135, 164-165
Tha Li (Thailand) 201
Tha Phabat District (Bolikhamsai) 83, 138, 150
Thai baht 6
Thai border 147, 159, 199, 201, 203
Thai Dam ethnic group 213
Thai visitors 2, 3
Thailand 79, 122, 147, 168, 203, 226
Tham Piew Cave 210
Tham Ting Caves 176
Thapangthong District (Savannakhet) 31, 100, 126, 196
Thaphabat District (Bolikhamsai) 32, 213
That 15, 36, 57, 66, 150, 162-164, 179, 182, 197
That Dam 15
That Luang 36, 44, 98, 115
That Luang Festival 6, 59-61
That Makmo 179
That Phabatphonsan 150
That Prathoum 179
That Sikhotthabong 164
Thatch 101
Thatheng District (Sekong) 205
Thathom District (Saisomboun) 189-190
Theaters 47
Theng (Vietnam) 184
Thong hai hin 208
Thongmisai District (Sayabouli) 200
Thoulakhom District (Vientiane) 40, 79, 105, 113, 118, 125, 131, 140, 142-143, 215
Thyrostachys siamensis 133
Thysanolaena latifolia 97
Tiger 143, 177
Tilapia 10, 51, 53, 72
Timber 86-89, 102, 200
Tin mining 165
Tire changing 129
Tithonia diversifolia 132
Tobacco 24, 112
Tonpheung District (Bokeo) 124, 148-149
Totems 146
Toulakhom District (Vientiane) 31
Toumlan District (Salavan) 139, 193
Tourism Authority of Thailand 150
Tourists 2-3
Tractors 201
Traffic lights 17
Tragulus javanicus 142

Trans-Asia Highway 123
Transliteration of Lao script 2
TRAVEL 116-129
Travel by Air 116
Travel by Rail 122
Travel by Road 123-129
Travel by Water 117-118
Traveling Salesmen 113, 205
Trays 103
Tree farming 86
Tree stumps 104
Trekking 174
Tribal Life 62-65, 168, 171, 186
Tribal settlement patterns 63
Trichoptera 137
Trimeresurus albolabris 139
T-shirts 1, 5
Tuk-tuk 54, 125, 218
Turkeys 85
Turtles 139
U.S. dollars 6
U.S.A. legacy 25-29, 36, 208, 210
U.S.A. program sponsorship 185
U.S.A. visitors 3
Udomsay, see Oudomsai
Udornthani (Thailand) 3
Unexploded ordnance (UXO) 25, 27-28, 144, 208
Update 3
Urban migration 112
Urban Problems 17-20
Urban renewal programs 8
UXO Lao 27, 144, 194
Vang Vieng 58, 92, 112, 217-218
Vang Vieng District (Vientiane) 58, 67, 81-82, 95, 97, 99, 105, 129, 133, 217-218
Vegetables 53, **75-78**
Vehicle sticker   cover, spine
Vertical Runway 11
Veunkham 74, 143, 157
Viangkham 213
Viangkham District (Vientiane) 31, 58, 214
Viangphukha District (Luang Nam Tha Province) 38, 65, 169
Viangsai 161
Viangsai District (Houa Phan) 74, 160-162
Viangthong District (Bolikhamsai) 152
Viangthong District (Houa Phan) 71, 77, 88, 109, 126, 130, 138, 163
Victory Gate 11
VIENTIANE, SEAT OF GOVERNMENT 9-21
Vientiane 2-6, 8, 23-24, 29, 31, 33-39, 41, 43-47, 51, 54, 56, 58-61, 65-66, 73-76, 79-82, 97-99, 102-104, 108, 110, 112, 114-116, 118-121, 124-125, 128-129, 134, 143, 219
Vientiane Capital 9-20, **21**, 36, 41, 45, 49, 54, 56, 57, 67, 72, 77, 102-103, 106, 112, 122, 130, 133, 137, 150
Vientiane Municipality 9
Vientiane Prefecture 9
Vientiane Province 7, 8, 31, 36, 40, 49, 58, 66-69, 72-73, 78-79, 81-82, 85, 90-92, 95, 97, 99, 105, 112-113, 118, 125-126, 129, 131-132, 134, 139-140, 142-143, 189, **213-218**
Vientiane Times vi, 3
Vientiane Times citations 3, 7, 25, 29, 30, 81, 87, 119,121-123, 136, 143-144, 147, 157, 189, 195, 199, 208, 211

Vietnam 144, 150, 184, 195, 226
Vietnam border 87,133, 144, 153, 173, 192, 194-195, 212
Vietnam visitors 3
Vietnam War 25-28, 208
Vietnamese salesmen 113
Vilabouli District (Savannakhet) 84, 195
Vindula erota 138
Visit Laos Year 1999-2000 campaign 3
Visit Muong Lao 3
Volleyball 43
Vung Tao 159
Wall hangings i, 4, 108-109, 160, 177, 180, end papers, back cover
War scrap metal 28, 154, 207, 209
Wasps 137
Wat 31-37
Wat Chanthabouli 35
Wat Haw Sin 36
Wat Inpeng 34
Wat Mai 178
Wat Naganimid 150
Wat Phiawat (Sieng Khouang) 209
Wat Phiawat (Vientiane) 34
Wat Phonsan 32
Wat Phosai Sayalam 34
Wat Phou 156
Wat Si Amphon 34
Wat Si Muang 35
Wat Sieng Lom 177
Wat Sieng Thong 34
Wat Sisaket 35
Water buffaloes 46, 67, 82, 169, 187, 190, 194, cover
Water lilies 99
Water shortages 55, 65, 159
Water throwing 54
Water towers 14, 18
Waterfalls 21, 40, 45, 55, 150, 155, 158, 160, 167, 170, 176-177, 192, 206, 211
Watermelon Stupa 179
Watermelons 79
Wattay International Airport Vientiane 1, 14, 24, 116
Weaving 4, **108-109**, 160, 162, 176-177, 180, end papers, back cover
Weddings 42
Welding 115
Whitewash 17, 23
Wickerwork 103
Wildlife 136-143
Wildlife habitat 144
Wine 92
Women's International Group bazaar 5, 47
Woodcraft 4, 5, 104-105
Wooden hangers 4
Wooden knockers 33
Woodworking 104-105
World Bank 7
World Heritage Site (UNESCO) 156, 178, 211
X listings, see S listings
Xaignabouly, see Sayabouli
Xaysomboun, see Saisomboun
Xiangkhoang, see Sieng Khouang
Yam bean 75
Yao ethnic group 162-163
Yuang Falls 40, 155
Zeltus amasa 138
Zoo 7, 140, 142-143, 215

These are the flags of the ten countries that now constitute the Association of Southeast Asian Nations, as shown on a souvenir shirt developed by the Lao Postal Enterprise (EPL). Can you name them? Hint: they are in alphabetical order by the names they use for themselves.*

The author, here seen at Houa Phan Province's mysterious menhirs, is a retired entomologist. During his years as a graduate student at Cornell University he participated in the Southeast Asia Program. The Southeast Asian portions of his career have spanned thirteen years, and included serving as a U.S. Peace Corps Volunteer in Thailand's National Malaria Eradication Project; doing research for a thesis on Thai flies; and researching flies as well as the transmission of dengue fever in Malaysia at the Institute for Medical Research and at the University of Malaya. He lived in Laos from 2001 to 2004, during which time he traveled overland for 80,000 kilometers on new roads, mountain tracks, deep mud, billowing dust, and river fords. He set foot in every one of the 141 districts in the country, photographing as he went. Some 1200 of his pictures appear here.

*Brunei, Indonesia, Kampuchea (Cambodia), Laos, Malaysia, Myanmar (Burma), Philippines, Singapore, Thailand, Vietnam